W9-BNK-694

LAW 101

AN ESSENTIAL REFERENCE FOR
YOUR EVERYDAY LEGAL QUESTIONS

BRIEN A. ROCHE, ATTORNEY AT LAW
JOHN K. ROCHE, ATTORNEY AT LAW
SEAN P. ROCHE, ATTORNEY AT LAW

sphinx
publishing

Copyright © 2009 by Brien A. Roche
Cover and internal design © 2009 by Sourcebooks, Inc.®
Cover images © Getty-Antar Dayal/brandXpictures

Sourcebooks and the colophon are registered trademarks of Sourcebooks, Inc.®

All rights reserved. No part of this book may be reproduced in any form or by any electronic or mechanical means including information storage and retrieval systems—except in the case of brief quotations embodied in critical articles or reviews—without permission in writing from its publisher, Sourcebooks, Inc.® Purchasers of the book are granted a license to use the forms contained herein for their own personal use. No claim of copyright is made in any government form reproduced herein.

First Edition: 2004

Published by: **Sphinx® Publishing, An Imprint of Sourcebooks, Inc.®**

<u>Naperville Office</u>
P.O. Box 4410
Naperville, Illinois 60567-4410
630-961-3900
Fax: 630-961-2168
www.sourcebooks.com
www.SphinxLegal.com

This publication is designed to provide accurate and authoritative information in regard to the subject matter covered. It is sold with the understanding that the publisher is not engaged in rendering legal, accounting, or other professional service. If legal advice or other expert assistance is required, the services of a competent professional person should be sought.

From a Declaration of Principles Jointly Adopted by a Committee of the
American Bar Association and a Committee of Publishers and Associations

This product is not a substitute for legal advice.

Disclaimer required by Texas statutes.

Library of Congress Cataloging-in-Publication Data is on file with the publisher.

Printed and bound in the United States of America.
POD — 10 9 8

Dedication

We dedicate this edition to a woman who holds the
dubious distinction of being the wife of one of the authors
and the mother of the other two.

Acknowledgments

I would be remiss if I did not acknowledge the input that many other people have had to this book. My paralegal, Pam Greenleaf, has reviewed this book several times with a fine-tooth comb and has provided invaluable input. My partner, Bob Johnson, provided a great deal of input. My secretary, Jovita Reynolds, typed the final draft. My two older sons have joined me as coauthors and have significantly contributed to all aspects of the book.

Brien Roche
May 2009
Alexandria, Virginia

Contents

Section Two: The Court System

Section Three: Areas of the Law

Preface

As the laws in this country become increasingly complex, people frequently ask, "What exactly *is* the law?" This book addresses what it means to say, "It's the law." Understanding how each type of law is formed and applied will help define that statement. The law is divided into: constitutional law, statutory law, case law, administrative law, and common law. This book serves as a guide to determining what is the law and how it may affect our everyday lives.

Our laws are derived from several different sources. Those sources are:

◆ the U.S. Constitution and state constitutions;
◆ statutes or ordinances passed at the local, state, or federal level;
◆ case law that is published by either state or federal courts (common law); and,
◆ administrative rules and regulations that are enacted by administrative agencies.

The law may take any of these forms. Understanding the scope of each form helps in understanding when the law found in those forms is binding in any given situation. An explanation of each of those different types of law and how they impact our lives is contained in this book.

The scope of this book is limited. There is no way that a book of this size can comprehensively summarize the law for all fifty states, as well as federal law.

Federal law is uniform throughout the entire United States. State law, however, may vary dramatically from one state to another. My law practice is confined to Virginia, Maryland, and the District of Columbia. Many of the examples that I have given in this book are related to legal principles derived specifically from those jurisdictions. If you have a specific legal problem, you should consult an attorney in your jurisdiction who can advise you on your specific legal issue.

Section One

*Where Our Laws
Come From*

Chapter One

Constitutional Law

The Constitution that most of us are familiar with is the U.S. Constitution. In addition to the U.S. Constitution, all fifty states have their own state constitutions. To some extent, these are modeled after the U.S. Constitution—but may vary from it. The state constitutions may give the people of that state greater rights than the U.S. Constitution bestows upon them, but it cannot restrict the rights guaranteed by the U.S. Constitution. The U.S. Constitution in that respect is supreme, but more importantly, the U.S. Constitution sets minimum standards that must be complied with by all governmental officers in dealing with the people.

The U.S. Constitution is divided into seven articles and twenty-seven amendments. The Constitution begins with the words:

We, the people of the United States, in order to form a more perfect union, establish justice, insure domestic tranquility, provide for the common defense, promote the general welfare and secure the blessings of liberty to ourselves and our posterity, do ordain and establish this Constitution for the United States of America.

The U.S. Constitution Is a Compact

The U.S. Constitution is a *compact*, or an agreement of the people of this land. It sets forth certain basic rights of the people that cannot be taken away and defines the powers of the governmental authority. The U.S. Constitution truly is the foundation of our entire legal system. Some people would say that the rights we enjoy in this country are natural rights, and that the Constitution is simply a clarification of those rights and a limitation on the power of the government to infringe on those rights. Others say that the Constitution itself is the actual source of the rights. But that theoretical argument is probably of little significance to the reader. What is important to remember about the Constitution is that it does set forth the essential composition of our government and how it can interact with us as citizens.

Try a quick test of your knowledge of constitutional law at this point. Suppose your next door neighbor breaks into your home looking for something that he thinks you may have stolen from him. The neighbor conducts a thorough and obviously unreasonable search of your premises without a warrant. Is that a *constitutional* violation?

Hopefully you said "no" to answer that question. The Constitution is a compact between the *people* and the *government*. Constitutional violations can only be committed by the government or its representatives. As such, one citizen violating the rights of another citizen is not a constitutional violation at the federal or state level. Your neighbor *has* violated state law, and he can be charged with that state law violation and also could be sued civilly for trespassing and for damaging your property.

It's the Law

Constitutional violations can only be committed by the government or its representatives.

The most important point to keep in mind regarding the U.S. Constitution is that it is the basic framework or foundation upon which our legislative, judicial, and executive branches are built. It defines certain basic rights that the people have and that no governmental authority can take away. The framers of the U.S. Constitution wished to define the authority of government and then place in the people all rights that were not specifically bestowed upon the government.

The Articles of the Constitution

Article One of the U.S. Constitution sets forth the powers of the U.S. Congress. It specifies that there shall be a House of Representatives and a Senate, and defines how their members shall be elected and compensated. It also sets forth general powers and limitations of those legislative bodies.

Article Two of the U.S. Constitution states that the executive power of the government shall be vested in the President. It then defines the extent of that executive power, how the president shall be elected, and what his or her qualifications for office shall be.

Article Three of the U.S. Constitution states that the judicial power of the United States shall be vested in the Supreme Court, as well as inferior courts Congress may establish.

The model created in the first three articles of the Constitution is a system of *checks and balances.* Each branch of government is considered to be equal, and each one in different respects has the ability to check and to balance the others. For instance, the legislative branch has the authority to enact legislation. That legislation is then sent to the president who, as the head of the executive branch, can veto the legislation. The legislative branch may then override that veto. If the law is passed (actually becomes law), then it can be reviewed by the judicial branch for purposes of determining whether it is constitutional and for purposes of interpreting the law. If the legislative branch, for whatever reason, does not like the interpretation imposed on the law by the judicial branch, then it can amend the law so as to expressly state how the law should be interpreted.

Article Four of the U.S. Constitution defines the concept known as *Full Faith and Credit,* which means that the public acts, records, and judicial proceedings of any one state shall be given full faith and credit in every other state in the union. This Article also defines the term known as *privileges and immunities,* which means that the citizens of each state shall be entitled to all the same privileges and immunities as the citizens of any other state. The privileges and immunities clause precludes one state from granting certain privileges or immunities to its citizens that would not apply to citizens of other states. For instance, Minnesota could not grant Jesse "The Body" Ventura the sole right to conduct wrestling matches in that state to the exclusion of all persons who were not citizens of Minnesota. To allow that would be a violation of the privileges and immunities clause.

Article Five of the U.S. Constitution provides for amendments to the Constitution.

Article Six of the U.S. Constitution states that this Constitution and the laws of the United States made pursuant to the Constitution shall be the supreme law of the land. That means that if there is any conflict between federal law and state law regarding an issue that the federal government has the right to legislate, then federal law will always be supreme.

Article Seven of the U.S. Constitution provides that nine states are needed to ratify the Constitution before it becomes effective.

The Bill of Rights

The first ten amendments to the Constitution are referred to as the *Bill of Rights*. They contain many of the most fundamental rights enjoyed by the American people.

The First Amendment states that Congress has no authority to make any law "respecting an establishment of religion or prohibiting the free exercise of religion." It further states that Congress can do nothing to restrict *freedom of speech* or *freedom of press*, or the right of the people to *peaceably assemble* and to *petition the government*.

The Second Amendment deals with the *right to bear arms*, but is written in the context of bearing arms as part of a regulated militia.

The Third Amendment states that the government cannot, in time of peace, *quarter soldiers* in a private home without the consent of the owner. In time of war, the government may only do so in a manner prescribed by law.

The Fourth Amendment deals with *unreasonable searches*. It expressly states that people shall be secure in their persons, houses, and papers from unreasonable searches and seizures by governmental authorities. It further states that search warrants may be issued only upon a finding of probable cause. That means there must be a determination made, based upon substantial, believable evidence, that the person to be searched has committed a crime or the place to be searched contains evidence of a crime.

The Fifth Amendment defines the concept known as *double jeopardy*, which means that a person cannot be tried twice for the same crime. (See Chapter 6 for more details.) That same Amendment further sets forth the right against *self-incrimination*—that a person cannot be made to testify against him- or herself. This Amendment also contains the foundation of the *Due Process Clause*, which states that a person cannot be deprived of life, liberty, or property without due process of law.

Due process is a critical concept to our entire legal system. It requires two things:

◆ A person must be given notice of the charges or claims made against him or her.
◆ A person must be given an opportunity to answer those charges or claims before he or she can be deprived of life, liberty, or property.

The Sixth Amendment provides for the *right to a speedy trial* and the *right to a jury trial* in a criminal proceeding. (See Chapter 6 for more details.) This Amendment further sets forth the *right to confrontation* in a criminal case, meaning that a person accused of a crime has the right:

◆ to confront the witness who is making the claim against him or her;
◆ to compel witnesses in his or her favor to appear in court and give testimony; and,
◆ to be represented by a competent lawyer in the defense of that criminal charge.

The Seventh Amendment establishes the right to have a jury trial in certain civil cases.

The Eighth Amendment prohibits *excessive bail* and disallows punishment that is deemed to be *cruel and unusual*. This Amendment has been used to argue against capital punishment and other forms of punishment over the years.

The Ninth Amendment states that just because certain rights are set forth in the Constitution does not mean they are the only rights people have. That is to say, whatever other rights the people have, they still retain.

The Tenth Amendment limits the power of the federal government by stating that powers not delegated to the United States Government by the Constitution and not prohibited by the Constitution to the states are expressly reserved to the states or to the people. The initial framers of the Constitution viewed the U.S. Government as a government of *limited authority*. Whatever authority was not placed in the United States Government rested with the states.

The Fourteenth Amendment

There are numerous other amendments passed over the years that are significant. Perhaps the most important of those is the Fourteenth Amendment—one of the post-Civil War amendments ratified in 1868. This Amendment contains several clauses, the most important of which is the so-called *Due Process Clause,* which expressly indicates that no state shall deprive any person of life, liberty, or property without due process of law.

You may recall that within the Fifth Amendment there is a due process clause. That due process clause, as is true of the first ten amendments, was deemed to be a restriction of federal power and not state power. This meant that the federal government could not deprive any person of life, liberty, or property without due process of law. That restriction, however, did not apply to the states until the enactment of the Fourteenth Amendment. Through the eventual interpretation of the *Due Process Clause* contained within the Fourteenth Amendment, most of the rights contained within the Bill of Rights were deemed to be no longer simply a restriction on federal power but also on state power. This means that those rights contained within the Bill of Rights apply to citizens not only when dealing with the federal government, but also when dealing with state and local governments.

The Fourteenth Amendment also contains what is known as the *Equal Protection Clause.* It states that governmental authority may not be used to deny any person equal protection of the laws. Over time, that equal protection clause was interpreted to preclude governmental authority from denying black citizens the same protection of the laws as was accorded to white citizens.

Other Amendments

All of the amendments are important. A brief description of the other amendments to the U.S. Constitution follows.

- The Eleventh Amendment states that federal courts do not have the authority to hear lawsuits brought by a citizen or non-citizen of one state against another state in the Union. (This is not to be confused with *diversity jurisdiction*.)
- The Twelfth Amendment deals with the functioning of the electoral college.
- The Thirteenth Amendment abolishes slavery.
- The Fifteenth Amendment extends the right to vote to all citizens.
- The Sixteenth Amendment allows for income tax to be imposed.
- The Seventeenth Amendment deals with the number of senators for each state and how vacant senate seats are filled.
- The Eighteenth Amendment enacts prohibition.
- The Nineteenth Amendment grants women the right to vote.
- The Twentieth Amendment deals with presidential succession and the convening of Congress.
- The Twenty-first Amendment repeals prohibition.
- The Twenty-second Amendment imposes limits on how long a person can serve as President.
- The Twenty-third Amendment allows the District of Columbia electors to vote for President and Vice President.
- The Twenty-fourth Amendment establishes the right of citizens to vote without being restricted by paying a poll tax. This is an Amendment principally designed to prohibit states from precluding certain citizens from voting by imposing financial restraints on them.

◆ The Twenty-fifth Amendment deals with presidential succession.

◆ The Twenty-sixth Amendment gives 18-year-olds the right to vote.

◆ The Twenty-seventh Amendment prohibits congressional pay raises from taking effect until the next election of representatives.

State Constitutions

Aside from the U.S. Constitution, each state within the Union has a state constitution. Those state constitutions may vary dramatically from one state to another. The key point to remember in regard to the state constitution is that it may bestow *additional rights* upon the citizens of that state, but it cannot restrict the rights guaranteed under the U.S. Constitution.

Chapter Two

Statutory Law

Statutory law falls into three categories—federal statutory law, state statutory law, and local statutory law. The federal statutory law is found in the United States Code. The state statutory law is found in the state code enacted by the legislative body that governs that state. Local statutory law is found in local codes and ordinances. Those local codes may be county codes, city codes, or town codes that are enacted by the local governing body.

Preemption

A general principle that applies to this statutory scheme is a principle known as *preemption*. When there is a conflict on a specific issue between federal statutory law and state statutory law, federal law will generally *preempt*, or *supersede*, the state law. That same principle applies in regard to a conflict between state law and local law. Local government cannot enact legislation that is contrary to the state statutory law. The logic behind this concept is that there has to be one entity that is supreme. For instance, it would be an absurd situation if the federal government passed an income tax law and then certain states decided that their citizens would not have to comply with that law. The American Civil War was fought in part over the issue of states' rights—whether the federal government was going to be supreme or whether the states were going to be supreme on the issue of slavery.

Codes

The federal statutory laws are found in the United States Code. The copy of the Code that most lawyers are familiar with is the United States Code Annotated. The term *annotated* means there are notations following the code section from court cases that have interpreted or applied that particular statutory code section. The annotations are frequently helpful in interpreting what the true meaning is of that statutory code section.

Most state codes are annotated and contain court decisions from both state and federal courts interpreting the various code sections. Local codes tend not to be annotated simply because the local governments that publish the local codes do not have the financial resources to annotate their local codes. Also, there tends not to be a great volume of case law interpreting local codes.

There is a shorthand abbreviation that is used for references to the United States Code. For instance, 28 USC §1392 is a reference to Title 28 of the United States Code Section 1392. The United States Code contains many volumes, like a set of encyclopedias. All of the titles are numbered sequentially on the binding of each volume. 28 USC §1392 would be found in one of the volumes marked Title 28. Within those volumes, §1392 would be found sequentially.

The state codes may have their own distinct numbering system. For instance, in regard to the Virginia Code, references to a code section would be to a specific numbered section such as Virginia Code Section 8.01-234. That is a reference to Title 8.01. Within that title, you would look for the code section designated as 234. Local codes may be designated in a similar fashion.

The volume of legislation that has been passed by the United States Congress is, in many respects, mind-boggling. There is federal legislation on virtually every issue. It is important to keep in mind, however, that the federal government, even though it seems to be involved in every aspect of our lives, is still a government of limited jurisdiction. You may recall from the section dealing with constitutional law that our founding fathers established the federal government as a government of limited authority with the understanding that whatever authority was not bestowed upon the federal government remained with the state governments. You would never guess that by looking at the volume of federal legislation.

The most significant limitation upon the authority of the federal government is to enact legislation in the criminal sphere. For instance, the federal government

> ## It's the Law
> *Whatever authority was not bestowed upon the federal government remains with the state governments.*

has no authority to pass a statute that prohibits homicide in your private home on private property. The federal government does have the authority, however, to pass a law prohibiting homicide on federal land, in a federal building, or against a federal officer. As such, most criminal prosecutions are initiated in the state courts under state law, because the authority of the federal government to enact criminal law truly is limited.

Example: *The dichotomy between federal and state law was found in the Rodney King case in Los Angeles, in which police officers were accused of beating a criminal suspect. Those police officers were first tried under state criminal laws and were acquitted (i.e., found not guilty).*

The federal government then stepped in and decided that those same police officers would be prosecuted under federal civil rights laws. The federal government had no authority to prosecute them for the crime of assault, since the crime in question did not occur on federal territory, did not involve a federal official, and did not involve a distinct federal interest as far as the assault only was concerned.

The federal government, however, has passed laws that make it a crime for certain persons acting in official governmental capacity to violate the civil rights of people. Those police officers were then prosecuted in the federal court under that federal law. It is in the criminal field that you see the authority of the federal government most clearly restricted in terms of its ability to enact legislation prohibiting certain types of crimes.

At first blush, it would seem that this is a violation of the double jeopardy *clause contained within the Fifth Amendment of the United States Constitution. It has been held, however, by the courts that it is not a double jeopardy violation since there are two separate sovereigns involved—the federal government and the state government. In addition, there were two separate offenses involved—one was the offense of assault under the state code and the other was a civil rights violation under the federal code.*

It's the Law

It is in the criminal field that you see the authority of the federal government most clearly restricted.

Local Codes

The impact of local codes is most often seen in regard to housing, traffic, and zoning issues. For instance, if you want to build a home of a particular type on a specific piece of property, the construction may have to meet certain zoning requirements in terms of height, size, and proximity to the boundary line. In areas where zoning regulations apply, you probably would not be able to build a ten-story home in a residential community with a building height limit of twenty-five feet. Likewise, traffic laws frequently are set forth in local codes, although those local traffic regulations have to be consistent with any state laws passed on those same issues. Again, the issue of preemption applies. For instance, an absurd situation would exist if every locality were allowed to decide whether a green light meant go or stop.

Chapter Three

Case Law

Case law is the law as stated in specific cases decided by courts. Case law is in written form, and generally contains a brief synopsis of the facts of the case, an analysis of the legal principles that apply, and a statement of the court's decision (what is generally known as the *holding* of the case). The holding is the crux of the decision rendered by that court. Insofar as that court has jurisdiction or authority to interpret the law, the holding then becomes law. Any language in the case decision other than the holding is surplus language, or what may be referred to as *obiter dictum* (or simply *dicta*). The *dicta* within a court decision is not binding law, but rather is simply utilized by that court to explain its rationale.

To fully understand the scope of case law and what effect it has upon our daily lives, it is necessary to understand the structure of the court system. In the United States there are two entirely separate and distinct court systems—the federal court system and the state court system. Each state has its own court system that is entirely separate and distinct from the federal system and from the court systems of the other forty-nine states in the Union.

Federal Courts

The federal court system is somewhat more integrated than the state courts because the federal courts do not necessarily recognize state boundaries in terms of their authority. The federal courts consist of the Supreme Court, circuit courts, and district courts.

The U.S. Supreme Court is the most important federal court. It sits in Washington, D.C., and is composed of nine judges, or *justices*, who are nominated by the president and then approved by the Senate. The sitting justices are all attorneys, and, in fact, most of them are former judges from lower courts who have been elevated to the U.S. Supreme Court. However, there is no requirement that a U.S. Supreme Court justice be an attorney.

The United States Supreme Court is a court of *discretionary appeal.* That means it exercises its discretion in deciding which cases it will hear. As a court of appeal, it does not actually try cases, it simply reviews legal briefs as submitted by attorneys or litigants. It hears oral arguments that are limited to an hour or two and thereafter renders a written decision. The U.S. Supreme Court does not actually hear from witnesses, hear evidence, or resolve factual disputes as might be done by a jury. Rather, it simply reviews the record presented from the trial that occurred in the lower court, and then determines whether there was a procedural, evidentiary, or constitutional error committed at the trial court level.

In order to have a case presented to the U.S. Supreme Court, the party who is requesting the hearing must first file a petition. If the petition is denied, the case will not be heard by the U.S. Supreme Court. If the petition is granted, the nine justices will hear the appeal and render a decision. Thousands of cases are appealed to the U.S. Supreme Court every year, but only a very small percentage of them are actually heard.

Example: *In the 2002 term, 8,255 cases were appealed to the U.S. Supreme Court, but the U.S. Supreme Court only issued written decisions in seventy-nine cases.*

The federal court system is essentially shaped like a pyramid. At the top of the pyramid is the U.S. Supreme Court. The U.S. Supreme Court is, as its name suggests, supreme and is final in the sense that it is the court of *last resort.* There is no higher court. Below the U.S. Supreme Court are eleven U.S. Circuit Courts of Appeals. The United States is divided into eleven numbered federal circuits, plus two additional circuits designated the D.C. Circuit and the Federal Circuit. (See map on p.18). Within each of those circuits is a U.S. Circuit Court of Appeals. These courts hear appeals from either the trial court below or from certain federal agencies that have a right of *direct appeal* to the U.S. Circuit Courts.

These U.S. Circuit Courts are somewhat similar to the U.S. Supreme Court in that they are simply courts of appeal. The U.S. Circuit Courts do not actually try cases—they do not hear evidence, the litigants do not testify in front of them, and they do not typically resolve factual questions as would be done by a jury. The U.S. Courts of Appeals simply review briefs submitted to them by attorneys, then hear oral argument from the attorneys, and thereafter render a written decision or issue an order either affirming, modifying, or overruling the decision from the trial court.

The following diagram is designed to show in a general framework the layout of the court system on both the federal level and the state level.

COURT SYSTEM

COURT	*FEDERAL SYSTEM*	*STATE SYSTEM*
Highest Court	U.S. Supreme Court	Name may vary from state to state, but frequently called Supreme Court.
Intermediate Court of Appeals	U.S. Circuit Court of Appeals	Name may vary from state to state.
Trial Court	U.S. District Court	Name may vary from state to state. Some states have a single-tiered trial court. Other states have a two-tiered trial court system, which means that there are two different levels—one being a higher trial court for more serious matters and the other being a lower trial court for less serious matters.

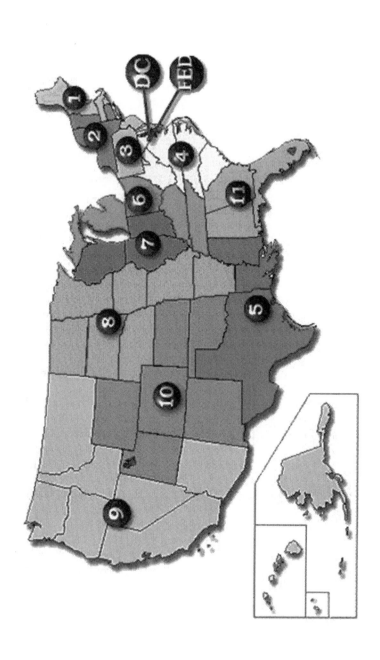

Below the U.S. Circuit Courts of Appeals are the U.S. District Courts, which are the trial courts within the federal system. The United States is divided into ninety-four federal districts. For instance, in the state of Virginia there are two federal districts: the Eastern District of Virginia and the Western District of Virginia. In the United States District Court for the Eastern District of Virginia, there are several different divisions that are part of that federal district. A division simply means that there is a courthouse located in that locality to serve the counties or cities within proximity of that courthouse.

The United States District Courts are presided over by United States District judges, who are nominated by the President to their position and then approved by the Senate. There may also be *magistrates* within the United States District Court, who are judicial officers with the authority to hear certain types of cases assigned to them by the United States District judge.

The United States District Court as a trial court is a *court of limited jurisdiction*, meaning that it has only limited authority to hear certain types of cases. In the criminal area, the United States District Courts can only hear cases that involve any federal crime (*i.e.*, a violation of federal law). For instance, referring back to the Rodney King case, the police officers in that case were charged with a violation of federal civil rights law. They were tried in a United States District Court before a United States District Court judge with a jury that was composed of citizens within that United States district.

United States District Courts, as courts of limited jurisdiction, can only hear cases that involve either a question of federal law (*federal question*) or that involve disputes between citizens of different states. This latter requirement, dealing with citizens of different states, is known as *diversity jurisdiction* in the federal courts. For example, a citizen of the state of Connecticut may sue a citizen of the state of Mississippi in the United States District Court of Mississippi relating to an automobile accident that occurred in Ohio.

Federal law not only requires that there be diversity of citizenship, but also that the amount sued for (the *amount in controversy*) be at least $75,000. As such, if you were involved in an automobile accident in the state of Texas while you were a citizen of Texas and the other party likewise was a citizen of Texas, you could not bring that suit in federal court because there is no diversity of citizenship. If, on the other hand, the other party to the automobile accident was driving a United States postal truck, the case would be brought in the United States District Court, since it is a claim against the U.S. Government based on a federal statute (*e.g.*, the *Federal Tort Claims Act*).

Types of Cases

It is important to make a clear distinction in your mind between criminal cases and civil cases. A criminal case is, in essence, a lawsuit brought by the government acting through a prosecutor against an individual who is accused of violating a criminal statute. For instance, if you deface a federal building, you may be charged with a federal crime in a federal courthouse. Or if you punch your next door neighbor in the nose on private property, you most likely would be charged with a violation of a state criminal statute. It would be tried in state court before a state court judge, and you would have the right to have a jury present, with that jury being drawn from the cities, counties, or towns where that court has jurisdiction. (Chapter 6 addresses the criminal process in both the state court and federal court systems in greater detail.)

It's the Law

A criminal case is, in essence, a lawsuit brought by the government acting through a prosecutor against an individual who is accused of violating a criminal statute.

A civil case, on the other hand, does not involve any criminal penalty. A civil case involves a claim for *monetary relief* or a claim for *equitable relief.* For instance, if you are injured in an automobile accident, you may have a right to sue that other party for monetary damages seeking compensation for your medical expenses, loss of income, and pain and suffering. In a claim seeking equitable relief, you are asking the court to order the other party to either do or not do something. For example, you may sue your next door neighbors to *enjoin*, or prevent, them from extending their home onto your private property. In that case, you are not asking for money damages but for an order to enjoin your neighbors from constructing their home on your private property. There are a wide variety of civil cases that may be instituted. (Chapter 5 addresses civil litigation in both the state and federal court system.)

State Courts

The state court systems vary dramatically from state to state. Some states have a single trial court. In these states, the trial court is generally referred to as a court of *general jurisdiction*, wherein all civil and criminal cases are initiated.

Other states have what is referred to as a *two-tier trial court* system. In the state of Virginia, the lowest trial court is the General District Court. That court hears all criminal *misdemeanor* cases and can also hear all civil cases wherein the amount claimed is less than $15,000. (A *misdemeanor* is a crime wherein the potential penalty is no more than one year in jail.) There are no juries in the General District Court. Any case that is heard in the General District Court may then be appealed to the Circuit Court, where the party bringing the appeal is entitled to a new trial (referred to as a trial *de novo*). In the Circuit Court either party can request a jury trial. The Circuit Court is a court of *general jurisdiction*, meaning that virtually any type of case can be brought within the circuit court.

Many states also have what is referred to as an *intermediate court of appeals*. That intermediate court of appeals is essentially the equivalent of the United States Circuit Court of Appeals, except that the state intermediate court of appeals only hears appeals from the state trial courts. These intermediate courts of appeals generally will hear any case that is appealed to them. However, in some states the intermediate courts of appeals are courts of limited jurisdiction and may have authority to only hear certain types of cases.

The highest court in most states is referred to as the Supreme Court, but some states may refer to their highest court by a different name. That high court may be a court of *discretionary appeal*, meaning that they exercise discretion as to which cases they will hear, much like the U.S. Supreme Court. These courts of appeal, whether they be intermediate or supreme, do not actually try cases, but simply review briefs and records submitted to them by the attorneys, then hear oral arguments and make a decision.

Case Law

The case law referred to earlier in this chapter consists of the *written decisions* of the various courts. Typically, trial courts do not generate case law. Even though a trial court judge may issue a written opinion (also called a *decision*) in a given case, that decision has very limited application. Decisions rendered by trial judges are only binding in regard to that specific case. They do not necessarily have any controlling effect upon any other trial judge within that trial court and do not have any controlling effect on any trial judge in any other trial court. Trial courts are the lowest tribunal and as such any written decisions rendered by trial court judges are of limited application.

Many cases decided by trial courts are decided by juries. Juries do not render written decisions explaining their analysis of the case, but rather simply render a verdict. That verdict in a civil case would be either in favor of the plaintiff or in favor of the defendant. If the verdict is in favor of the plaintiff and there is an amount of money being sought by the plaintiff, then the jury would fix the amount of the monetary award (*i.e.*, value the damages). If there is no jury deciding the case, then the judge may enter a verdict or a judgment order fixing the amount of damages or granting one party the form of relief that is sought.

Federal Court Decisions

Case law for the most part comes from *appellate* courts. The appellate courts may be intermediate courts or they may be the high court of that state or court system. For instance, there is an abundance of case law rendered by the U.S. Circuit Court of

Appeals. Likewise, there is a wealth of decisions rendered by the United States Supreme Court.

The decisions of the appellate courts are contained within various bound volumes published by different law publishing companies. A written decision rendered by a United States District Court judge may be published in legal books known as the *Federal Supplement* (abbreviated F. Supp.).

Example: *A decision rendered by a United States District Court judge is generally referred to by the name of the parties, e.g., Jones v. Smith, 317 F. Supp. 2d 820 (N.D.IL. 2004). That case would then be found in volume 317 of the Federal Supplement Second beginning on page 820. The parenthetical means that it is a decision from a United States District judge in the Northern District of Illinois that was rendered in 2004.*

NOTE: The volumes are put into series and when they reach a certain number, generally 999, the numbering begins again at one. That is why you will find a 2d or 3d in the citation.

Decisions rendered by a United States Circuit Court of Appeals are found in law books known as the *Federal Reporter*. For instance, a decision rendered by the United States Circuit Court of Appeals for the Ninth Circuit could be reported at 356 F.3d 121 (9th Circ. 2004). That citation means that the decision was rendered by the United States Court of Appeals for the Ninth Circuit in 2004 and can be found in Volume 356 of the Federal Reporter Third Series at page 121.

Decisions from the United States Supreme Court may be reported in three different reporting systems, all of which are published by different publishing houses. For instance, a decision from the United States Supreme Court would frequently be referred to as *Jones v. Smith* 535 U.S. 85, 125 S. Ct. 25, 159 L. Ed. 2d 125 (2004). That decision would be found in any one of those three volumes with the first volume being referred to as the United States Reporter, Volume 535, page 85. That same decision can also be found in the

Supreme Court Reporter, in Volume 125, page 25, and would also be found in the Lawyer's Edition Second Series in volume 159, page 125. The year refers to the year when the decision was rendered.

State Court Decisions

Written decisions rendered within the state court system are found in regional reporters. The publishing house that is responsible for publishing state court decisions has essentially divided the United States into regions. For instance, Illinois is contained within the North Eastern Region. As such, a decision by the Illinois Supreme Court that is reported in written form could be found both in the state reporter, known as the Illinois Official Supreme Reporter, and also in the regional reporter, known as the North Eastern Reporter. The decision of *Jones v. Smith* from the Supreme Court of Illinois discussed earlier would be reported under the same name with the following citation: 208 Ill. 2d 450, 804 N.E.2d 480 (2004). The decision then would be found in volume 208 of the Illinois Official Supreme Reporter at page 450 and would also be found in the regional reporter known as the North Eastern Reporter at volume 804, page 480. Again, the year refers to the year when the decision was rendered.

Written decisions from trial courts at the state court level frequently are not published by any publishing house. To the extent they are available at all, they may only be available within that local court house. Some states have adopted trial court reporting systems wherein certain written decisions that are presented to them may be published. In the state of Virginia there is a publication known as Circuit Court Opinions, which consists of written decisions made by circuit court judges in the state of Virginia. Those decisions, however, are only published if either the judge or one of the attorneys forwards that written decision to the publishing firm.

Courts either at the state or federal level are charged principally with resolving disputes that are presented to them and, in that context, rendering interpretations of state or federal statutes or state or federal constitutional provisions. Any decision rendered by a trial court judge is subject to being reviewed and potentially overturned by the appellate court that has appellate jurisdiction over that trial court. For instance, in the federal system, any decision rendered by a United States District Court is subject to appeal to the United States Court of Appeals for that circuit. The United States District Court judge may have rendered a written decision. That decision then can be reviewed by the judges in the United States Circuit Court for that circuit, and those judges on the circuit court can either agree or disagree with the decision from the United States District Court. The decision rendered by the United States Court of Appeals likewise may be appealed to the United States Supreme Court. If the U.S. Supreme Court exercises its discretion and decides to hear the case, then the U.S. Supreme Court can either uphold or reverse that decision.

At the state court level the same procedure applies. Any decision rendered by a trial court can be appealed to the appellate court that has jurisdiction. The appellate court can then either uphold or reverse the trial court decision. The high court within that state generally has the last word on those cases that are initially tried within that state. However, if the case involves an issue of federal or constitutional law, then the U.S. Supreme Court can decide to hear a case from the state court system.

The Status of the Court

The importance of case law from various courts, to some extent, has to be evaluated based upon the status of the court that rendered the decision. This refers to the precedent value the case holds over other courts.

For instance, a decision rendered by a trial judge in the Hanover County Superior Court in North Carolina may be of great interest nationwide, but it is not binding on anyone other than the parties in that particular case. If that case, however, is appealed to the North Carolina Court of Appeals and a written decision is rendered, then that case law becomes binding to every person in North Carolina as the law of the state. If that case is then appealed to the North Carolina Supreme Court, then the decision rendered by the North Carolina Supreme Court becomes the law of North Carolina and is binding upon all litigants in the North Carolina State Court System.

If that case involved a constitutional or federal issue, it may be further appealed to the U.S. Supreme Court. A decision by the U.S. Supreme Court is binding upon the entire nation.

In the federal system, a decision rendered by a United States District Court judge is typically only binding upon the litigants in that case. However, if that case is appealed from the United States District Court to the United States Court of Appeals for that circuit, then the decision rendered by that United States Court of Appeals becomes binding upon all of the persons within that federal circuit. For instance, the Fourth Circuit Court of Appeals includes the states of Maryland, North Carolina, South Carolina, Virginia, and West Virginia. Any decision rendered by the United States Court of Appeals for the Fourth Circuit is binding upon all persons within that five state area.

It is quite possible that the United States Circuit Court for the Eleventh Circuit could decide a case with similar issues and come up with an opposite conclusion. Typically, when a conflict exists between circuits the issue will be presented to the U.S. Supreme Court to decide how to resolve the conflict between the circuits.

Chapter Four

Administrative Law

Another facet of the law is what is referred to as *administrative law*. At both the state and federal level, there are administrative agencies. Most of those agencies are part of the executive branch of government. As discussed in the material dealing with constitutional law, our government is divided into three branches—the executive branch, the judicial branch, and the legislative branch.

The executive branch is headed by the president at the federal level and by the governor at the state level. The judicial branch at the federal level is headed by the chief justice of the U.S. Supreme Court. At the state level, the Judicial branch is headed by the chief justice of the highest court of that state, which in most instances is referred to as the Supreme Court (although in some states, it may be referred to as the Court of Appeals).

Within the legislative branch, there typically is no one person who is the head of that branch. At the federal level, the legislature is *bicameral*, meaning that it consists of two bodies. Those two bodies are the House of Representatives and the Senate. The Speaker of the House is the leader of that legislative body. The *President Pro Tempore* is the leader of the Senate. At the state level, there may be the same general type of organization within the legislative branch.

You may be asking yourself, *What do the above comments have to do with administrative rules or regulations?* Although most administrative rules and regulations are set forth by administrative agencies within the executive branch, there may be administrative agencies within the judicial branch or the legislative branch that could set forth rules and regulations of their own.

The administrative agencies that most of us are probably familiar with are federal agencies like the Food and Drug Administration, the Department of Justice, the Department of Commerce, the Department of Agriculture, and the Federal Communications Commission. Some of these federal agencies are *cabinet-level* agencies, meaning that the heads of those agencies are members of the President's cabinet.

Others may be considered to be independent agencies. For instance, the Federal Election Commission is an independent agency that has the specific responsibility of overseeing compliance with the federal election laws by presidential candidates and other candidates at the national level. Another independent agency is the Nuclear Regulatory Commission, which is charged with the responsibility of overseeing the use of nuclear power in the nonmilitary arena.

These agencies generally have the authority to issue *regulations*. These regulations in some instances may be referred to as *rules*. Although there is a technical distinction between a rule and a regulation, for purposes of this discussion they are treated as being one and the same. These administrative agencies are created by acts of Congress and are given a specific purpose as set forth in the U.S. Code. The agencies are also given the authority to write and publish rules and regulations that will govern their conduct.

Rule-Making Process

The rule-making process consists of the following four steps.

1. The agency publishes proposed rules.
2. Members of the public are given the opportunity to comment on those rules.
3. The rules may be revised based upon the public's comments.
4. The final rules are enacted.

The document where these rules are published is known as the *Federal Register*. The Federal Register is a publication put out by the Government Printing Office that contains all of the proposed and adopted rules and regulations of the federal agencies.

As discussed earlier, there may be administrative agencies within the legislative and judicial branches of government. For instance, the General Accounting Office is an independent administrative agency created by Congress and charged with investigating all matters related to the receipt, disbursement, and use of public money. At the state level within the judicial branch of government there may be an administrative agency, known as the state bar, charged with the responsibility of administering and supervising the legal profession. As an administrative agency within the judicial branch of government, a state bar is subject to the control of the highest court of that state.

The regulations that are adopted by administrative agencies have the effect of law. They are designed to expand on laws created by legislative bodies. The legislative bodies that enact the statutory law try to be as precise as possible in terms of writing the statutes. However, the statutes are often somewhat general because the legislative body simply does not have the expertise or, in some cases, the time to enact statutes that deal with all of the nitty-gritty issues that may arise within that subject area. The administrative agencies generally have the expertise and the time to publish regulations that are much more precise and that deal with the nitty-gritty issues that the agency confronts.

> ### It's the Law
> *The regulations that are adopted by administrative agencies have the effect of law.*

The regulations published by the administrative agencies are designed to be an explanation and an elaboration of the statutes that the agency is charged with enforcing. Theoretically, there should never be a situation in which there is a conflict between what the statute says and what the regulations set forth by the agency say. If there were such a direct conflict, then the statute would be controlling. The regulations are designed to flesh out the statutory scheme. You may think of the statutes as being the skeleton and the regulations as being the meat on the bones.

Code of Federal Regulations

At the federal level, all regulations are published within the *Federal Register*. They are also contained within a document known as the *Code of Federal Regulations* (C.F.R.). The C.F.R. can be found in a law library and is generally organized in numerical fashion to correspond (to the extent possible) with the statutory code sections that they are designed to interpret and expand upon.

State Rules

These rules and regulations can be very important. Suppose you wanted to assert a claim against a motel owner because of carbon monoxide poisoning that occurred while you were in the motel. The type of claim that would be asserted would be a civil claim (law claim) for money damages based upon the negligence of that motel owner. There may, however, be regulations published by the state agency that control the motel/hotel industry that set forth certain standards as to how motels are to maintain gas producing appliances to prevent carbon monoxide poisoning. The regulations published by that state agency could be extremely helpful in pursuing a civil claim against that motel owner.

Rules for the Legal Profession

Members of the legal profession are governed by rules and regulations published by their profession. Within every state there is an agency or entity that is responsible for publishing rules that govern the conduct of attorneys. Those rules of conduct are generally referred to as *disciplinary rules*. If an attorney violates a disciplinary rule, he or she may be disciplined by the state bar and subjected to certain sanctions. For example, if you were represented by an attorney and found that the attorney had done something that you considered to be highly improper, you might want to look at the disciplinary rules to see if there is something set forth there that might govern the particular behavior in question.

There are also rules of procedure designed to provide some uniformity as to how lawsuits proceed. Rules of civil procedure:

◆ define what should be contained within a set of suit papers initiating a lawsuit (also called a *complaint*);

- ◆ define how a complaint is to be served;
- ◆ set forth what affirmative defenses may be raised by a defendant;
- ◆ set forth a variety of rules governing the discovery process; and,
- ◆ set forth the procedures by which a judgment of a court may be reviewed by the trial court.

Rules of criminal procedure govern how a defendant is to be dealt with in terms of the initial charging, his or her right to be informed of the charge, what rights he or she may have in terms of discovery, and how the eventual trial will proceed.

Legal Analysis

This concludes the section dealing with the sources of the law. To fully understand what the law is, you must know whether the law referred to is constitutional law, statutory law, case law, or administrative law. In some respects, there is a certain pecking order or hierarchy that might be applied to those different sources of the law. If a particular activity is either allowed or disallowed under the Constitution, then no statutory law, case law, or administrative law can overturn that. That is not to say, however, that all constitutional rights are necessarily absolutes.

It's the Law

Your constitutional rights can be restricted to some extent by state or local laws.

For instance, people have a constitutional right to peaceably assemble, but for purposes of maintaining public order the government may require that you obtain a permit to conduct that peaceable assembly on public property. Simply because you want to peaceably assemble by calling a demonstration on Fifth Avenue in Manhattan does not mean that you have an absolute right to do that during the middle of rush hour. In that sense, your constitutional rights can be restricted to some extent by state or local laws.

In looking at a legal issue or question, the general checklist of things that you would want to ask yourself is as follows:

❏ Is there some constitutional provision that may be involved?
❏ Is there any statutory law that may be controlling?
❏ Is there any case law dealing with this issue, and, if so, what court am I going to look at in terms of determining the source of that case law? (If the issue is one that involves provisions of the U.S. Constitution, then the U.S. Supreme Court is the ultimate decision maker in those questions. Look at case law from that court, as well as case law from any of the lower federal courts. If the issue is simply one involving state statutory law, look at case law from the highest court of that state.)
❏ Are there any administrative rules or regulations that may be applicable?

Section Two

The Court System

Chapter Five

Civil Litigation

As discussed in Chapter 3, there are two types of cases—criminal and civil. A federal judge may one day conduct a complex civil trial and the next day preside over a routine federal criminal case. There is no distinct demarcation between civil court and criminal court within the federal court system. However, there may be a clear demarcation between the two in some states. There may be a specific court that is known as the criminal court, wherein only criminal cases are heard. The important thing to keep in mind is that the civil system is entirely separate and distinct from the criminal system. Indeed, the rules that apply to one in many instances have no application whatsoever to the other. This chapter explains civil justice in both the state court and the federal court systems. (Chapter 6 addresses the criminal justice process in both the state court and federal court systems.)

Civil Justice in the State Court System

Within the civil justice system there are two types of claims that can be presented to and resolved by the court—law claims and equity claims. A *law claim* is a claim for money damages. *Money damages* means that the party bringing the suit (the plaintiff) is requesting that a monetary judgment be awarded against the party who is being sued (the defendant). Another type of claim that can be litigated in the civil justice system is an *equity claim*. In some states an equity claim is referred to as an *equitable claim* or a *chancery claim*. Equity claims are claims wherein the party bringing the suit is not necessarily asking for judgment for a monetary amount, but is asking the court to direct the other party to either do something or not to do something.

Example: *A law claim might arise from an automobile accident where one party is injured and claims the injury is due to the fault of the other driver. The lawsuit may be filed requesting the court to award a monetary amount against the party that is accused of being at fault.*

> *An equity claim might arise when one neighbor is seeking to enjoin (or prevent) another neighbor from building an extension of their home onto the first neighbor's property. To prevent that type of encroachment, a lawsuit would be filed requesting an injunction. If the court granted that request, then an injunction would be issued preventing that activity.*

Divisions within a Court

Within the civil justice system there may be several divisions or offices of the court dealing with different types of issues. There may be a landlord/tenant division, a small claims division, a domestic relations division, a probate division, and a tax division. Each of those divisions deals with the types of claims associated with their name. For instance, the landlord/tenant division will deal with landlord/tenant disputes, including evictions by landlords or complaints by tenants involving failure to comply with building code requirements.

The small claims division may deal with any type of claim within a jurisdictional monetary limit. The small claims division is a type of people's court, wherein lawyers are typically not allowed and the strict rules of evidence may not apply. The domestic relations division deals with domestic matters, including divorce, custody, alimony, child support, and adoption. The probate division deals with estate matters and guardianship matters. Finally, within a civil court there may be a general civil division that would hear all claims other than the ones mentioned above.

Filing Suit

Any person can walk into a courthouse and file a lawsuit. The party bringing that lawsuit is referred to as the *plaintiff*. The party being sued is referred to as the *defendant*. The initial document filed with the court to initiate a lawsuit may have different names, depending upon the jurisdiction where you are filing. Typically, the initial document filed with the court to initiate a civil claim is referred to as a *complaint*. In any complaint, you can ask for either *legal relief* or *equitable relief*. If the claim being pursued is a legal claim, then the damages being requested would consist of *compensatory damages* and perhaps *punitive damages*.

> ## It's the Law
> *Compensatory damages are designed to make a person whole from the loss he or she has suffered.*

Compensatory damages are damages that are designed to compensate the plaintiff for his or her injuries. To put that another way, compensatory damages are designed *to make that person whole* for the loss he or she has suffered as a result of the conduct of the defendant. Punitive damages, on the other hand, are designed to punish the defendant for egregious conduct. Punitive damages are rarely awarded, and normally when they are awarded they are carefully reviewed by the court to determine the appropriateness of the award.

Serving the Suit Papers

Once a lawsuit has been properly filed, that complaint has to be served upon the defendant. It is served either by the local sheriff, a special *process server*, or any other person authorized by law. The form of service is typically *personal service*, meaning that the complaint and any other accompanying court process (documents) issued by the clerk of the court has to be served on the defendant in person. Some states authorize what is referred to as *substituted service*, meaning that in some instances the complaint may be delivered to a member of that defendant's household or may even be posted on the front door of the residence where the defendant is believed to live.

If the defendant cannot be found through one of those means, then there may be other forms of substituted service allowed by state law. These consist of service upon the Commissioner of the Department of Motor Vehicles in regards to an automobile accident, and, in some instances, service upon the Secretary of State when the defendant is believed no longer to be living in that state. These other forms of service are governed by state law, and thus vary from state to state.

Response by the Defendant

Once the lawsuit has been filed and the complaint has been properly served, the defendant has a designated period in which to respond. That period of time normally ranges anywhere from twenty to thirty days. The defendant may respond by filing a motion or by filing an answer. The different types of motions that may be filed by the defendant in response to the complaint would be motions raising issues of lack of jurisdiction, failure to properly state a claim, or certain other affirmative defenses.

A motion based upon a *lack of jurisdiction* is a statement that the court in which the suit was filed does not have jurisdiction—the authority—to hear the claim. Another type of motion that may be filed is a motion to dismiss for *failure to state a claim*, which means that the defendant is saying that even if everything stated in the complaint is true, it still does not constitute a basis for a lawsuit against the defendant.

Other types of *affirmative defenses* that may be raised through a motion would be such defenses as the statute of limitations, res judicata, release, accord and satisfaction, and several other such defenses. If a *statute of limitations* defense is raised, the defendant is claiming that the suit was filed too late and is therefore barred by the statute of limitations. If a motion is filed based upon *res judicata*, the defendant is claiming that this claim has already been adjudicated once and it cannot be litigated again. If the defendant raises the defense of *release* or *accord and satisfaction*, there has been some sort of settlement reached in regard to the claim and therefore the reassertion of the claim is barred.

If no motions are filed within the time allowed after service of a complaint, the defendant is to file an answer. That *answer* is supposed to respond to each of the numbered paragraphs of the complaint so that the plaintiff knows exactly what issues are going to be contested. In addition, the defendant may be called upon to raise any affirmative defenses in that answer. An affirmative defense may be any of the defenses mentioned above that could be raised in the form of a motion or other such defenses that would constitute an automatic bar to the claim asserted.

Discovery

Once the answer to the complaint has been filed, most civil claims allow for what is called discovery. *Discovery* is designed to allow each party to ask the other party what they know about the claim that has been asserted, who any relevant witnesses may be, and to identify any relevant documents. Discovery may come in several different forms.

It may come in the form of written *interrogatories*, consisting of written questions that either party may send to the other. These have to be answered in writing and under oath. The discovery may also consist of *requests* for documents and inspection, meaning that the party issuing the request wishes to see documents in the possession of the other party, or may wish to inspect certain things in the custody or control of the other party.

In addition, there may be *requests for admissions*, which are written statements the other party is required to either admit or deny. The purpose of requests for admissions is essentially to narrow the issues of contention in the case so that each party knows exactly what they are fighting over.

There may also be depositions. A *deposition* is an oral examination that is conducted in the presence of a court reporter. The purpose of a deposition is to have an opportunity to orally examine the other party or witnesses so that there are no surprises at trial. The overall purpose of this discovery process is to make sure that each side has ample opportunity to discover the claims or defenses of the other party so that at the time of trial, each party is fully aware of what the other party intends to present.

Pretrial and Trial

After the conclusion of the discovery process, there may be a *pretrial conference* with a judge. The purpose of that pretrial conference is to identify the remaining issues that need to be decided and to attempt to resolve any outstanding legal issues prior to the trial. In addition, some courts conduct what are referred to as *settlement conferences*. These conferences may be conducted by neutral mediators and are designed simply to allow the parties to come together in an informal setting to discuss settlement. Those settlement discussions are generally confidential and if the case does not settle, anything said during those settlement conferences cannot be used against the other party.

If the case is not settled it will be scheduled for trial. It may be tried either before a judge or a jury. Juries are picked from the general population of that city, county, or jurisdiction where the court sits. Every state has different rules as to exactly how juries are chosen, but typically they are chosen from the voter registration rolls and property ownership rolls of that jurisdiction. In some jurisdictions, they may also be drawn from the Department of Motor Vehicle rolls.

Voir Dire

If the case is to be tried before a jury, then the first stage in the trial is *voir dire*. *Voir dire* literally means "to speak truthfully." It is an opportunity for certain questions to be asked of the potential jurors to determine whether they know anything about the case, whether they know any of the parties, whether they have any interest in the outcome of the case, or whether they may have any particular bias or prejudice for or against either party. *Voir dire* is typically conducted by the attorneys, although in some courts it may be conducted by the judge. Once the *voir dire* is completed, the parties have the opportunity to strike (dismiss) all or some of those jurors they feel would not be receptive to their case.

In addition, some jurors may be stricken *for cause*. For example, if a juror indicates that, based upon what she has heard about the case, she has already made up her mind, typically she is going to be stricken for cause because she comes to the case with a predisposition.

Opening Statement

Once a jury has been chosen, the court will allow both parties to have *opening statements*. The purpose of opening statements is to allow the attorneys to give the jury a road map of where the case is going to go. Opening statements are not intended to be argumentative, but are intended to simply be a recitation of the facts that will be presented during the course of the trial.

Presentation of Evidence

Once the opening statements have been completed, the plaintiff will present his or her evidence first. That evidence comes in two forms—the presentation of testimony from witnesses and the presentation of documents or other tangible things for the jury to review. At the conclusion of all the plaintiff's evidence, the defendant has the right to make a motion to dismiss or to strike the plaintiff's case based upon any number of legal theories. This type of motion is a statement by the defendant saying that even if the plaintiff's evidence is to be believed, it is not sufficient to justify a judgment being entered against the defendant. The court normally will rule on such a motion at that time. Typically, that type of motion is denied. If the motion is denied, the defendant then has the right to present his or her evidence.

At the conclusion of the presentation of all of the defendant's evidence, the defendant may renew his or her motion to strike or for a directed verdict. In addition, the plaintiff may make a motion to strike any defenses and to request the court enter judgment against the defendant as a *matter of law*. That type of motion is a statement by the plaintiff that even if what the defendant says is true, he or she still has no *bona fide* defense to the claim, and therefore there is nothing for the jury to decide.

It's the Law

The function of a jury is to hear evidence when there is a factual dispute, to evaluate that evidence, and then to render a decision based on it.

It is important to keep in mind that the function of a jury is to hear evidence when there is a factual dispute, to evaluate that evidence, and then to render a decision based on it. If there is no true factual dispute, then there is nothing for a jury to decide and the court (judge) will make the decision.

Jury Instructions

At the conclusion of all of those motions—if they are denied—the jury will be instructed by the court what the law is in the case. Those instructions may be oral or they may be given to the jury in writing. The jury will then be instructed to consider all the evidence, the jury instructions, and then render a verdict.

Before they begin their deliberations, however, the jury will hear from the attorneys one more time in the form of *closing arguments*. The purpose of closing arguments is to give the attorneys one last opportunity to argue their respective positions on the case in order to persuade the jurors to vote in their favor.

The size of a jury may differ from jurisdiction to jurisdiction. The size of a jury in a civil case is usually anywhere from five to twelve people, but the parties can agree to have fewer jurors.

Verdict

Any decision rendered by a jury is normally expected to be unanimous in a civil case. The jury reviewing the evidence is required to apply the principle that the plaintiff has the *burden of proof*. The plaintiff, being the one who is bringing the claim, has the burden of proving his or her case by what is referred to as the *preponderance of the evidence* (the greater weight of the evidence). If you think of a scale that is evenly balanced, and if a feather were placed on one side of that scale, then that feather's weight would constitute a preponderance of the evidence. If the plaintiff tips the scales in his or her favor by so much as a featherweight, then the plaintiff has met his or her burden of proving the case by a preponderance of the evidence.

Sometimes people ask: *What does it mean to prove something?* Something is proven by presenting evidence in support of it. Any evidence may be sufficient to prove something. One witness testifying that he or she saw you run a red light may be sufficient to establish your fault in an auto accident case, even though you presented ten witnesses who said that the light was green.

Post-Trial Motions

Once a jury verdict is entered, either party has a right to *make post-trial motions*. Those post-trial motions will typically come in the form of a motion for a new trial, a motion to decrease the size of a jury verdict, or, in some instances a motion to increase the size of the jury verdict.

Judges are reluctant to disturb a jury verdict. The traditional thinking has been that once a jury has spoken, that statement is final. If, however, the jury obviously disregarded the instructions of the court or returned a verdict that is clearly excessive or inadequate, the court has the authority to set aside that verdict (and, in some states, to actually alter that verdict).

Motions for a new trial must be based on some procedural error committed by the trial judge. For instance, if the trial judge admitted evidence that should not have been admitted, allowed an attorney to say something to the jury that was inappropriate, or improperly instructed the jury on an issue of law, then there may be a basis for a motion for new trial.

Appeal

If either party feels as though he or she has not been dealt with fairly by the trial court, that party has a right to appeal the decision to the next highest court within that state's court system. Although each party has a right to appeal, the court may be a court of discretionary appeal, and may decide not to hear the case. (The particular structure of the different appellate courts has been previously discussed. See Chapter 3.)

An appeal is a very laborious process. In order to properly present an appeal, the *transcript* of the trial proceeding may have to be prepared. That transcript is prepared by a court reporter. The court reporter expects to be paid for the preparation of a transcript. The preparation of a transcript frequently costs several thousand dollars. In addition, the party bringing the appeal has to present a legal argument (in the form of a brief or memorandum) to the appellate court stating why the trial court's decision is in error.

The parties are not allowed to present new evidence on appeal. Instead, they are bound by the record created at the trial court level. Anything that was not properly presented or properly objected to at the trial court level is not going to be considered on appeal. An appeal is not an opportunity to re-try the case. It is simply an opportunity to request a higher court to review and correct an error made by the trial court. If a reversible error is found, the case is sent back to the trial court for a new trial or, in some instances, the appellate court reverses the trial court's decision and enters a new judgment.

Court Rules

Most courts have adopted rules of procedure and rules of evidence. Those rules of procedure may be contained, to some extent, in the state code (in which case the procedural rules in essence become statutory law), or they may be in a formal set of rules referred to as the rules of procedure. In the federal court system, there is a set of rules referred to as the *Federal Rules of Civil Procedure*. Many state courts have adopted similar sets of rules of civil procedure.

In addition, there may be a set of rules referred to as the *rules of evidence*. In the federal court system, there is a formal set of rules referred to as the *Federal Rules of Evidence* that has been written by the Judicial Conference. Those Federal Rules of Evidence apply in federal court. At the state court level, many states have adopted their own state rules of evidence. Those rules are designed to govern the admissibility of evidence in that state court system.

Evidence

As previously defined, *evidence* is the presentation of testimony from witnesses and the presentation of documents or physical things for the jury to review. The rules of evidence govern how those things may be admitted into evidence. For something to be admitted into evidence technically means that the jury is allowed to hear it or see it. If it is not admitted into evidence, then the jury should not see or hear it. If, by chance, they have heard or seen evidence that was not properly admitted, they will be instructed to disregard that evidence. The rules of evidence are designed to provide some degree of reliability to the evidence that is presented in the courtroom. These rules can become very complex.

> ## It's the Law
> *The rules of evidence are designed to provide some degree of reliability to the evidence that is presented in the courtroom.*

The principal form in which evidence is presented is putting a witness on the witness stand and having him or her respond to questions from the attorney who has called that witness. The testimony rendered by that witness is considered to be evidence. The jury may rely upon that evidence to decide the case. The testimony presented by one witness may be sufficient to convince a jury to rule in favor of the party that called that witness, even though the other party may have called ten witnesses who presented contrary testimony.

Rule on Witnesses

If you have ever been in a courtroom in which multiple witnesses are potentially going to testify, you may recall the judge asking whether there is a request for a rule on witnesses. The *rule on witnesses* means that witnesses who have not testified should not be in the courtroom. That rule does not apply to the parties to the litigation. This means the plaintiff and the defendant in a civil case both have a right to be present, even though they may testify as witnesses. However, witnesses who have not yet testified may be excluded from the courtroom until they testify. In addition, this rule on witnesses may be extended to prohibit anyone from talking to witnesses about what is going on in the courtroom until that witness gives his or her testimony. A violation of that rule on witnesses may result in a witness being excluded from testifying. The purpose of this rule is to prevent one witness' testimony from being influenced by what another witness has said in the courtroom.

Direct Examination

The party that calls a witness to testify is required to ask that witness *nonleading questions*. That form of examination, called *direct examination*, is intended to allow the witness to testify rather than to have the attorney testify. If the attorney were allowed to ask *leading questions* (questions that suggest the answer within the content of the question) then in essence the attorney is testifying and not the witness. An example of a leading question would be "Isn't it true that you beat your wife?" That question, by its very content, suggests that the answer is yes—that the witness does beat his wife. That type of questioning is not allowed on direct examination. A nonleading form of that same question would be "What do you know about your wife having been beaten?"

The general purpose of direct examination of witnesses is to allow the witness to explain what he or she knows. If that witness provides testimony that needs further explanation, then the attorney can ask the witness to simply explain the answer.

Cross-Examination

The purpose of *cross-examination*, on the other hand, is to allow the adverse party (the party who has not called the witness) to try to pin that witness down. The witness is not typically allowed to explain his or her answers on cross-examination.

A skillful cross examiner will ask only questions in the form of *Isn't it true that...?* That type of questioning is intended to elicit a simple yes or no answer and to not allow the witness to explain answers in any detail. This form of questioning is called *leading*. If the witness wishes to explain the answer or if the attorney who initially called the witness wishes to have the witness explain the answer, then that attorney will have the opportunity on *redirect examination* (the examination that takes place after the cross-examination).

The general format by which questioning of witnesses is conducted is:

◆ first, by direct examination, in which nonleading questions are asked by the attorney calling the witness;

◆ second, by cross-examination by opposing counsel, frequently through the use of leading questions; and,
◆ third, by redirect examination, in which the party that originally called the witness may ask more nonleading questions, allowing the witness to explain any answers that may have been given on cross-examination.

Cross-examination is generally limited by the *scope* of the direct examination. If, on direct examination, the witness was only asked a limited number of questions about limited issues, then the cross-examination must be limited to those issues. The cross-examination may not go beyond the general scope of the direct examination.

Impeachment

Once a witness has been put on the witness stand, he or she may be *impeached*. To impeach a witness means to contradict him or her in some manner or form, or to otherwise undermine his or her credibility. A witness may be impeached by presenting contrary statements that he or she has made on prior occasions about the issue in controversy; by showing that he or she has some particular bias or prejudice against the other party; or, by attacking the witness' character by showing that he or she has been previously convicted of a criminal offense constituting a felony or a crime of moral turpitude. (A *felony* is a crime for which a person may be imprisoned for more than a year. A *crime of moral turpitude* is a crime that involves lying, cheating, or stealing.)

Normally, in a civil case, general character evidence is not admissible. The court in a civil action does not want to hear evidence about how good a person the plaintiff or the defendant may be. However, that type of testimony may be allowed in a criminal action to show the character and reputation of the defendant who has been accused of the crime.

Competency of Witness

The *competency of a witness* to testify may frequently become an issue. Generally, any witness within the *age of reason* is considered to be competent, provided that witness has not been declared incompetent by a court. The age of reason varies depending upon the maturity and intelligence of the witness, with age 7 generally being a cutoff point. Between ages 7 and 14, it is a matter for the trial judge to determine whether the child is of sufficient sophistication to testify. A person is declared incompetent by a court if there has been a judicial determination that he or she is deficient in mental capacities to the point where he or she cannot conduct his or her own affairs and needs to have someone else appointed as a guardian. If a person has been declared incompetent, then he or she may not be able to testify.

Other issues of competency may arise in terms of taking an oath. Some people maintain that they cannot take an oath because of their religious beliefs. Normally, that is resolved by having the person affirm that they will tell the truth rather than having them state that they will tell the truth *so help me God*.

Privileges

In the course of litigation, it is not uncommon for one party to raise an objection based upon *privilege*. There are several different privileges that exist within the law. The *husband/wife privilege* precludes either spouse from testifying against the other based upon what they learned from the other spouse during the course of the marriage. If a husband tells his wife that he has just murdered the next door neighbor, then the wife may be precluded from repeating that statement in a court of law.

One of the privileges that is at the foundation of our legal system is the *attorney/client privilege*. When a client retains an attorney, anything that client says to the attorney is deemed to be privileged and cannot be repeated by the attorney without the consent of the client, unless the communication involves proposed criminal activity. For instance, if a client tells his attorney that he is about to blow up a building, the attorney—under the law of most states—must advise him of the possible legal consequences, urge him not to commit the crime, and advise him that the attorney must reveal his intention to the authorities unless he abandons the proposed criminal activity. If the client confesses to his attorney that he blew up a building, the attorney is bound by the attorney/client privilege not to disclose that information.

In the case of the attorney/client privilege, the privilege belongs to the client, not to the attorney. If the client wishes to divulge those communications, then he or she may do so. The attorney, however, may not divulge those communications without the consent of the client, unless the client has already divulged them on his or her own. Some states also recognize other types of privileges, wherein communications made by one person to another may not be divulged without the consent of the person to whom the privilege belongs. (Such privilege exists in regard to the *physician/patient relationship* and the *priest/penitent relationship*.)

Burden of Proof

As previously stated, the plaintiff has the *burden of proof* in a civil case. There are different burdens that apply in different types of cases. Generally, in a civil case, the burden of proof is what is referred to as *the preponderance of the evidence*—the greater weight of the evidence. Recall the example of tipping the scales by a featherweight. If the plaintiff tips those scales by so much as a featherweight, then his or her burden of proof based upon a preponderance of the evidence has been met.

In some civil claims, however, the burden of proof may be somewhat higher. In particular, regarding fraud claims, the burden of proof is generally considered to be what is called *clear and convincing* evidence. That burden of proof or standard of proof is higher than simply a preponderance of the evidence. If you were to think of a preponderance of the evidence as being something more than 50%, then clear and convincing evidence would be a level of proof in the range of seventy-five to perhaps as high as 90%.

Another term that is used in criminal cases is that of *proof beyond a reasonable doubt*. That is a level of proof that even goes beyond clear and convincing evidence, and probably is more in the range of 90%. (See Chapter 6.)

It is probably misleading to try to ascribe numerical figures to any of these standards of proof, since they really are not susceptible to numerical classification. These numerical classifications are merely designed to provide some illustration of the different levels of burden of proof.

Presumptions

Within the law of evidence, there are certain *presumptions* that may arise on occasion. A presumption is a recognition that if one particular fact is proven, then a second fact is inferred or assumed from the first.

> **Example:** *If I prove that a child is under the age of seven, then a presumption arises that the child is incapable of negligence. That is, having proved first that the child was under seven, the court then recognizes a presumption that the child cannot be guilty of negligence.*

This presumption may be unrebuttable. A different presumption may exist as to a child between the ages of 7 and 14. This presumption is considered to be a *rebuttable presumption*. If it can be shown that the child is of sufficient sophistication, intelligence, and experience that he or she can understand the nature of his or her acts and is capable of committing a negligent act, then the presumption may be rebutted.

> ### It's the Law
> *A presumption is a recognition that if one particular fact is proven, then a second fact is assumed.*

There are a number of other presumptions that exist in the law. A person accused of a crime is presumed to be innocent. That presumption must be overcome by the government by presenting evidence of criminal behavior. If a person holds the power of attorney for another individual and profits from that relationship, then there is a presumption that his or her profiting from that relationship is fraudulent. The basis for that presumption is that, as the attorney in fact or holder of a power of attorney for an individual, a person has a great deal of power over that individual and can manipulate the assets or activities of that individual.

A presumption of death from an absence of seven years may also arise. If a person disappears and is not seen or heard from for a period of seven years, then he or she is presumed dead.

Another presumption that is frequently referred to is the presumption of knowledge of the law. As a citizen of this country, you are presumed to know the law. Obviously, no one can know all of the laws. However, common sense should tell you that if you are about to engage in behavior that is questionable, then you may need to check to see whether that behavior is illegal. If you then engage in that behavior, you cannot raise a defense that you did not know the law, because you are presumed to know the law.

Relevance

The principle criteria of admissibility is that the evidence must be relevant. *Relevance* means that the evidence that is being offered tends to prove or disprove an issue in the case. If the issue in the case is whether you ran a red light, evidence that shows that the traffic light was not properly functioning at the time of the accident is relevant and typically would be admissible. Likewise, evidence of the cycle of nearby traffic lights and your speed as you traveled from a nearby intersection to the intersection in question may all be relevant to whether the light was red when you entered the intersection. All of those facts tend to prove or disprove whether you ran that red light and therefore are relevant.

> ## It's the Law
> *Relevance means that the evidence that is being offered tends to prove or disprove an issue in the case.*

Some evidence may be relevant but it is so highly prejudicial that the court determines that it should not be admitted. In tort claims, most courts have determined that evidence of insurance is not admissible because it is too prejudicial. If a jury knew that a defendant was insured, then the jury's verdict might be higher simply because of that. Accordingly, most courts have determined that evidence of a defendant being insured is not admissible even though it may be relevant.

Direct and Circumstantial Evidence

Evidence, in general terms, can fall into two broad categories. There is *direct evidence* and *circumstantial evidence*. Direct evidence consists of witnesses testifying to things within their personal knowledge, or it may consist of documents, pictures, or other things that directly prove a particular thing. For instance, a person testifying, "I saw the wolf attack the chicken coop," would be direct evidence.

Circumstantial evidence may be thought of as indirect evidence, or evidence that leads to a particular conclusion although there is no direct testimony, document, or thing that proves that event. Going back to the example of the wolf attacking the chicken coop—if no one actually saw the attack happen, but you see the wolf's footprints around the chicken coop and the dead chickens, then you may conclude that the wolf is the one who killed the chickens, even though no one actually saw it happen.

Physical Evidence

Documents and physical objects are frequently offered as exhibits or as evidence at trial. The first inquiry in regard to any document or other physical object is whether it is *authentic*. A document or object is authentic if it has been proven to be what it appears to be. If a will is presented to the court as an exhibit and is offered as the will of John Jones, then before that document can be entered into as evidence (shown to the jury) a witness will need to confirm that it is the will of John Jones and that the document bears his signature. That type of testimony establishes the authenticity of the document—simply that it is what it appears to be.

From a common sense point of view, lay people looking at that may say that it has the name at the top indicating that it is the Last Will and Testament of John Jones, it bears the signature of John Jones, and the signature appears to be authentic. Based upon all of that, common sense would suggest that the document is what it appears to be—the Last Will and Testament of John Jones. The court, however, normally requires more than simply the appearance of validity. Typically, a witness will need to testify that the document is in fact the Last Will and Testament of John Jones and the witness may have to testify as to how he or she knows that is so.

Once the authenticity of a document has been established, there may be other objections that could be made regarding that document. Any objections as to relevance and privilege will have to be dealt with.

Hearsay

A more common objection, however, is *hearsay*. The hearsay objection may arise not only in regard to documentary evidence, but also in regard to testimonial evidence (the testimony of witnesses). Generally defined, hearsay is an out-of-court statement that is offered for its truth value.

Example: *The plaintiff makes a statement at the scene of an accident saying "I am at fault." If it were to be offered as truth in court, would it be considered hearsay? Looking at the definition of hearsay as being an out-of-court statement that is offered for its truth value, the statement would be hearsay. The statement was made out of court (it was made at the accident scene) and it is being offered for its truth value (to prove that the plaintiff was at fault at the time of the accident because he said so).*

The general purpose of the hearsay rule is to exclude evidence that may not be reliable. Another reason for the exclusion of hearsay evidence is that its presentation denies the other party the right to cross examine the person who is making the statement. If, at the scene of an accident, a police officer makes a statement to the effect that the plaintiff was at fault for the accident, that statement is hearsay if offered as evidence in court because it was stated out of court and is offered for its truth value. If the police officer does not testify at trial, then obviously he or she cannot be cross-examined about that statement. It would be unfair to allow either party to repeat that statement in court because the witness making the statement is not present to be cross-examined about it. If, however, the police officer does testify at trial, then it is possible that, under certain circumstances, he or she may be confronted with that prior statement and asked to explain it.

As indicated above, hearsay evidence is not generally admissible, but there are a number of exceptions to the hearsay rule. For example, when the plaintiff stated that he was at fault, the statement was hearsay. However, the court may still admit it on the grounds of it being an exception to the hearsay rule because it is an *admission of a party* to this particular action. The exceptions to the hearsay rule are very extensive—so extensive that some people might say that the rule itself now has no meaning.

Experts

An expert witness is simply a witness who has expertise in a particular area, whose testimony the court has determined may assist the jury in understanding the issues of the case and therefore fairly deciding the issues. Expert testimony has been abused over the years in that it is sometimes presented on issues that do not require expert testimony. The rule of thumb for the admissibility of expert testimony is that it must relate to a subject matter that the jury might have difficulty understanding without expert testimony. The expert must assist the jury in understanding the issue. In a medical malpractice case in which there is an issue as to whether the surgery should have been conducted one way or another, the jury needs to hear expert testimony from medical doctors as to how the surgery should have been conducted. The jury does not have the expertise to decide that issue on its own, and therefore must hear from medical experts who will educate the jurors as to what the medical issues are and how the surgery either should have or should not have been conducted. Typically, if one party presents expert testimony, the other party will present contradictory expert testimony. It is then up to the jury to decide which of those experts they believe and to render a verdict.

Certain types of expert testimony have been ruled inadmissible by some courts. For instance, in some jurisdictions, expert testimony of how a particular automobile accident may have occurred is considered to be inadmissible because that is normally considered to be something that a jury can understand and determine on its own, without the aid of expert testimony.

There is a tendency within the legal profession to offer expert testimony on as many issues as possible in order to bolster the claim or defense being asserted. Recently, many courts have taken a somewhat dim view of that tendency and have endeavored to restrict the admissibility of expert testimony. The reasoning is that in many of these types of cases, the jury has sufficient expertise or common sense to understand and resolve the issues.

Civil Justice in the Federal Court System

The federal court system is quite different from the state court system. You will recall from what was said previously that the federal courts are courts of limited jurisdiction. On the other hand, the state courts are courts of general jurisdiction, or, to put it another way, virtually of *unlimited* jurisdiction. The term jurisdiction in this sense refers to *subject matter jurisdiction*—the types of claims that the court has the authority to hear.

There are some claims arising under federal law that can be asserted only in federal court, but the general rule is that virtually any type of civil claim (under state or federal law) can be brought in the state court system. That is not true of the federal court system. In order to bring a civil claim in the federal court, there are certain requirements that have to be met. There are two ways to bring a civil claim into federal court. You can bring a *diversity* claim or you can bring a claim involving a *federal question*.

Diversity Jurisdiction

A *diversity claim* is one wherein the parties are of diverse citizenship. A citizen of the state of Connecticut may sue a citizen of the state of Massachusetts in the federal court in Massachusetts. That difference or diversity of citizenship establishes one of the elements of a diversity claim. The diversity claim, however, must also involve a monetary controversy in which the amount at stake is in excess of $75,000 (not including any interest or any attorneys fees that may be claimed).

The civil jurisdiction of the federal courts is legislated by Congress. Congress has chosen to limit the overall civil jurisdiction of the federal courts. The logic is that civil litigants can always go into state court to resolve their disputes, and as such the federal courts should be reserved only for certain types of disputes. Disputes between citizens of different states may be subject to some local or regional prejudice if brought in state court, and therefore Congress has decided that these types of civil claims, provided they meet the monetary amount set forth above, can be brought in federal court in order to avoid the potential prejudice or bias.

Federal Question Jurisdiction

The second way of bringing a civil claim into federal court is by suing under a federal statute or a federal constitutional provision. For instance, if you file a civil rights claim against your employer, even though you may be a citizen of Ohio and you employer may be a citizen of Ohio, you can still bring that claim in federal court because the claim is brought under federal law. Likewise, if you pursue a claim against a defendant under a theory involving a violation of your constitutional rights, then that type of claim may be brought in federal court because it is founded upon a federal constitutional issue.

Unlike diversity claims, federal question cases do not have any monetary jurisdictional limits. That is, the discrimination claim that you bring against your employer may only be worth $100, but you can still bring that claim in federal court.

Personal Jurisdiction

In order to file suit against a person in the state of Massachusetts, for example, either in state or federal court, you have to assert and be able to prove that the court (state or federal) has *personal jurisdiction* over that defendant. Personal jurisdiction can be obtained in a number of different ways.

- ◆ If the defendant *committed the alleged wrong* in the state of Massachusetts, then that would give the courts (state or federal) within that state personal jurisdiction over him or her.

- ◆ If the defendant *lives* in the state of Massachusetts, then the courts (state or federal) in that state would have personal jurisdiction over him or her.
- ◆ If the defendant has engaged in a course of conduct wherein he or she has *substantial contacts* with the state of Massachusetts and the claim in question "arose out of those contacts," then that may likewise give the courts (state and federal) personal jurisdiction over him or her in the state of Massachusetts.

The concept of personal jurisdiction is entirely separate and distinct from the concept of *subject matter jurisdiction. Subject matter jurisdiction* of the federal courts (in terms of civil claims) must be founded upon diversity or a federal question. That relates exclusively to what is called subject matter jurisdiction. Personal jurisdiction deals with the issue of whether the court has authority over that defendant to litigate that claim. The concept of personal jurisdiction is founded on the idea that it would be unfair for a citizen of California to have to litigate a claim in Massachusetts unless that citizen of California had done something that would constitute some *substantial contact* with the state of Massachusetts that gave rise to the claim in question. The mere fact that a federal court may have subject matter jurisdiction to litigate your claim does not necessarily mean that it has personal jurisdiction over the defendant to litigate that claim.

> ## It's the Law
> *Personal jurisdiction deals with the issue of whether the court has authority over a particular defendant.*

State Court vs. Federal Court

Lawyers frequently argue over the respective merits of bringing a civil claim in state court versus federal court. Some lawyers maintain that it is always to the advantage of the plaintiff to litigate a claim in federal court for the following reasons.

♦ The Federal Rules of Evidence typically are a bit more lenient and, therefore, more favorable to a plaintiff than are the state rules of evidence.

♦ The federal courtrooms are much grander and larger than the typical state courtrooms; therefore, juries are likely to be more impressed with a case brought in federal court and more likely to return a verdict favorable to the plaintiff.

♦ Federal judges are sometimes considered higher caliber than state court judges.

Those reasons are very subjective, and there are probably as many lawyers across the nation who feel that it is better for a plaintiff to file suit in state court than in federal court. In any event, since the plaintiff initiates the lawsuit, the plaintiff has the opportunity, to some extent, to choose the forum. Even though a suit may be initiated in state court, if the federal subject matter jurisdiction requirements have been met, then the defendant may *remove* that case from state court to federal court.

> **It's the Law**
>
> *A federal court may have subject matter jurisdiction, but no personal jurisdiction, over the defendant.*

Once a case has been initiated in federal court, the process that is followed is much the same as what has been described previously in the state court system. The particular procedural rules that are followed in federal court may differ from what are followed in state court, but the basic procedure is much the same once the lawsuit has been initiated.

When hearing a diversity case, a federal court is, in essence, sitting as if it were a state court. The federal judge who is called upon to make rulings of law has to apply the pertinent state law that governs that transaction. If a citizen of Connecticut sues a citizen from Massachusetts in a federal court in Massachusetts for an automobile accident that occurred in the state of Connecticut, then the federal judge in Massachusetts is going to apply Connecticut law to that claim. Massachusetts law on the particular issues in question may be markedly different than Connecticut law.

A federal judge, however, who hears a federal question case typically is going to apply federal law, since the claim itself arose under federal law.

Even though a federal judge may be called upon to apply state law in a diversity claim, he or she is still bound by the Federal Rules of Procedure, which govern the civil procedure in that court system. He or she is also bound by the Federal Rules of Evidence, which are the rules that govern the admissibility of evidence in the federal court system. As such, a federal judge, when sitting in a diversity claim, is called upon to apply a number of different types of law—both state law and federal law—to different aspects of the case.

Chapter Six

Criminal Law and Procedure

There are several players in the criminal justice system—the police, the prosecutors, the judges, the parole and probation officers, and the *accused*, who is also called the defendant. Criminal prosecutions are typically initiated by the police by making an arrest. That arrest may be made as a result of a crime witnessed by a police officer or as a result of an investigation by the police. Once the police have made an arrest, the person arrested will begin to wind his or her way through the criminal justice system.

To describe the journey through the state criminal justice system (and for the most part, the federal system as well), the best place to begin is at the beginning. As with every aspect of the legal system, the beginning is the Constitution. The most frequent encounter with constitutional law is found in the criminal context. Criminal law and procedure, to a great extent, *is* constitutional law.

Constitutional Protections

The criminal process can be initiated by both state and federal prosecutors. The Bill of Rights (the first ten amendments to the Constitution) initially only restricted the power of the federal government and was not considered to have any application to criminal prosecutions in state court. But over the last fifty years, there has been a process of *selective incorporation*, wherein the rights guaranteed to defendants in federal criminal prosecutions have been selectively incorporated into state prosecutions.

Today, virtually all the rights set forth in the Bill of Rights apply not only to federal criminal prosecutions, but also to state criminal prosecutions. As such, a defendant's right to remain silent, the right to competent counsel, the right to confront his or her accusers, the right to be free from cruel and unusual punishment, and most of the other rights set forth in the Fourth, Fifth, Sixth, and Eighth Amendments have been made applicable to defendants charged with crimes in the state court system.

Many of the rights associated with a criminal prosecution are rights that come into play before an arrest is ever made. The Fourth Amendment says that you have a right to be free of *unreasonable police searches and seizures*. The police cannot stop you while you are walking down the street unless they have some reasonable justification for believing that you either have committed a criminal offense or are about to commit a criminal offense. If a police officer sees you walking down the street engaging in some unusual behavior, stops you to question you about this, and sees a conspicuous bulge under your coat that looks like it may be a pistol, then he or she may detain you and pat you down to determine if it is in fact a pistol. If it is a pistol and you are not allowed to be carrying such a concealed weapon, then you may be arrested.

Suppose a police officer receives a report that a bank has just been robbed and hears a description of the perpetrators broadcast over the police radio. If that police officer feels that you fit the description, then he or she may stop you and ask where you have been, where you are going, and request your identity. If the police officer is not satisfied at that point that you are not the suspect, he or she may even take you back to the scene of the crime to see if you can be identified by any of the witnesses. If you are then identified by one of the witnesses, you will be arrested.

A police officer, however, may not stop you and detain you while you walk down the street simply because you look suspicious or unsavory. Instead, he or she must have some reason that can be *articulated* that would cause a *reasonable person* to conclude that you have committed some criminal offense or are about to commit a criminal offense.

You have probably heard the saying *a man's home is his castle*. Indeed, that is true insofar as police searches are concerned. The

It's the Law
Generally, the police need to have a search warrant to conduct a search of your home.

police cannot randomly come into your home and conduct a search. Generally, the police need to have a search warrant to conduct a search of the premises. In certain emergency circumstances, they may be allowed to come into the premises and conduct a search. This is only allowed if it is necessary in order to accomplish an arrest of a person whom they believe has committed a crime or if it is necessary to prevent the destruction of evidence. If time permits, however, the police are required to obtain a warrant issued by a judge or magistrate authorizing the search and entry into a home.

Exclusionary Rule

A rule that has evolved over the years (and that is the subject of a good deal of controversy) is the so-called *exclusionary rule*. The *exclusionary rule* states that the courts will exclude evidence that was obtained as the result of an unreasonable search or seizure. The exclusionary rule is a rather general one, and over the years the courts have applied several exceptions to the exclusionary rule.

It's the Law
The intent of the exclusionary rule is to control police behavior.

The intent of the exclusionary rule is to control police behavior. It is felt that if the police realize that evidence they obtain in violation of someone's constitutional rights cannot be used in a criminal prosecution, they will control their behavior from that point forward, assuring that the constitutional rights of defendants are observed. The battle over the exclusionary rule has raged for nearly forty years, with some people arguing that it makes no sense to allow the criminal to go free simply because the police have bungled. People on the other side of the issue argue that the only way that the police can be controlled is by excluding evidence that they obtain illegally.

In order for a defendant to rely on the exclusionary rule, he or she must assert and prove that he or she has *standing* to challenge the alleged constitutional violation. This requirement of standing, or having an appropriate interest in the outcome of the case, is a general requirement for asserting any constitutional right. An example of where a defendant would not have standing arises when an illegal seizure of narcotics in the home of Defendant A leads to the subsequent arrest of Defendant B at another location. The narcotics in that case could not be used in evidence against A, because A has standing to object to the illegal arrest. The narcotics could be introduced against B, as B has no standing to object because it was not his home that was illegally searched and he was not the one who was illegally arrested. In that case, B would not have standing to raise a constitutional objection in order to exclude the evidence.

Criminal Procedure

Once a person has been arrested, the arresting officer is allowed to search that person and to search the area within arm's reach of that person. Anything that is found as a result of that type of search may be used against the defendant. Likewise, if there is some illegal substance or item that is within *plain view* of the officer while he or she is lawfully in the premises, then that substance or item may be seized and used against the defendant.

Vehicle searches are frequently the subject of controversy. When a motor vehicle operator is arrested and taken to the police station, his or her vehicle is typically impounded. The police are then authorized to conduct an *inventory search* of the vehicle. Since the vehicle has come into their possession, it is in the interest of the police to determine whether there are any items of value in that vehicle, so that they are not later charged with a misappropriation of those items. They typically will conduct an inventory search of the vehicle and if there is some illegal substance or material found in the vehicle, it could be the basis of a criminal prosecution.

Probable Cause

The general criteria for making an arrest is what is referred to as *probable cause*. Probable cause arises when there is sufficient evidence to cause a reasonable person to believe that the accused probably committed the crime in question. The key word is *probable*. That is, the accused is more likely than not to have committed the crime in question.

The police may rely upon a variety of different sources of information to arrive at probable cause. For instance, a police investigator who relies upon an informant that has been used in the past regarding drug activities may determine that there is probable cause that narcotics are being sold at a particular location. That may justify not only the issuance of a search warrant for those premises, but also the arrest of the persons inside the premises if narcotics are found. Probable cause may also be founded upon police surveillance, wherein the police have actually seen suspicious activities going on at a particular location. Many things may justify the issuance of a warrant and a search of the premises.

Warrants

In the criminal field, there are two different types of warrants that may be issued—arrest warrants and search warrants. An *arrest warrant* is an order issued by a judge or magistrate authorizing the arrest of a particular person for a particular crime. A *search warrant* is an order issued by a judge or magistrate authorizing the police to conduct a search of a specific premises looking for specific objects. Although the police do not always need to have a search warrant before conducting a search of a premises, it is generally preferred that they do, especially if time permits. In some circumstances, however, time does not permit the police to go to the local courthouse, find a judge who has time to review the situation, and obtain a search warrant. In those types of emergency circumstances—when evidence is about to be destroyed or when the crime is in progress—the police may enter the premises and conduct a search without a warrant.

If a search warrant has been issued, then the warrant may actually indicate when the search is to be conducted. Typically, when the search warrant is to be served and executed is a matter of discretion for the police. Once the police have arrived at the premises, they are expected to announce their entry. However, if they have some reasonable cause to fear that evidence is being destroyed or that the police themselves may be in danger as a result of announcing their presence, then the police may enter without notice. Once the police have entered the premises, anyone in the premises is detained pending the completion of that search. If illegal materials or the items that are sought are found in the premises, and if there is probable cause to believe that the persons on the premises have something to do with the crime at issue, then they may be arrested and charged with a criminal violation.

Sometimes the police may request a citizen to *consent* to a search either of their person or of their premises. Nobody has to give such consent. If a person does consent to the search of his or her physical person or his or her home, it is considered to be a consensual search and the police do not need a warrant.

Police sometimes are called upon to utilize various types of surveillance techniques, consisting of wiretapping and electronic eavesdropping. That type of surveillance is controlled by specific state or federal statutes and as a general rule a warrant is necessary before the police can engage in that type of activity.

Miranda **Rights**

One of the most notable decisions of the U.S. Supreme Court involving criminal procedure is the *Miranda* decision. The *Miranda* case involved the Fifth Amendment to the U.S. Constitution and related specifically to the rights of a criminal suspect after he had been detained by the police. The *Miranda* case held that the Fifth Amendment right against self-incrimination meant that a person had the right to be advised of his or her right to remain silent, right to counsel, and right to terminate any police interrogation once it has begun after being arrested, before he or she could be questioned by the police.

It's the Law

If the defendant spontaneously volunteers information, there is no Miranda *requirement.*

Miranda does not require that these rights be given to every person who is arrested. Frequently, a person is arrested and the police have no intention of asking him or her any questions about the alleged criminal activity. If, however, the police do begin asking questions about the alleged criminal activity, then they are required to give the *Miranda* rights. If those rights are not given and the defendant divulges information in response to police questioning, that evidence may be excluded at trial. If the defendant spontaneously volunteers information, there is no *Miranda* requirement and therefore the evidence would not be excluded.

The scope of *Miranda* has been altered by different courts and generally is now held to apply not only to persons who have been arrested, but also to persons who have become the focus of a police investigation. Even if a suspect has not been arrested, if he or she has become the focus of a criminal investigation and the interrogation is what is deemed to be *custodial*—taking place in a police station or another type of police environment—then the police must give the *Miranda* rights to that suspect before conducting their interrogation.

A suspect or a defendant can waive the right against self-incrimination and is free to speak to the police about his or her involvement in criminal activities. Experienced police officers normally require that waiver to be in writing or to be recorded so that there is no question that the suspect or defendant is voluntarily and knowingly waiving his or her rights.

Judicial Review of Arrests

Once a person has been arrested and charged by the police, then his or her case is reviewed either by a prosecuting attorney or a magistrate. *Magistrates* are judicial officers who fulfill some of the functions of a judge but do not have the complete authority of a judge. The purpose of having the case reviewed by the prosecuting attorney or the magistrate in the early stages of the process is to determine whether the police had probable cause to believe that the person had committed the crime in question. If the magistrate or prosecuting attorney makes that determination, then normally the case will move on to the next stage.

Also in the early stages of the process, the court will set *bail*. Bail is typically set by a magistrate or a judge who considers the seriousness of the offense and the likelihood of the defendant fleeing the jurisdiction, and then establishes a monetary amount that must be paid to secure the defendant's appearance at all subsequent court hearings. Bail can be paid in a cash amount or may be paid in the form of security against a piece of real estate. More often, it is paid by the posting of a *bond* written by a bail bondsman.

A bond issued by a bail bondsman is a type of insurance policy with the court as the beneficiary of that policy. The defendant who obtains the bond from the bail bondsman pays a premium for that bond, which normally is a certain percentage of the face amount of the bond. If the defendant does not appear at subsequent court proceedings, then the bondsman has to pay that bond amount to the court. The bondsman then will frequently use a bounty hunter to go out and find that defendant and return him or her to the court so that the bondsman can redeem (get its money back) its bond.

The Eighth Amendment provides that *excessive bail shall not be required*. That is a rather loose standard and indeed the amount of bail that will be set by the court is a very subjective matter.

Prosecutors

The *prosecutor* is a governmental employee charged with the responsibility of bringing suspects to trial. Prosecutors are attorneys. Of all the government officials that you may ever encounter, prosecutors are probably the most powerful. They have absolute discretion in deciding to prosecute an offense or not to prosecute an offense. If a murder has been committed in your hometown and a suspect has been arrested by the police, the prosecutor must decide whether the case will be taken to the next level. The decision of the local prosecutor is not subject to review by any other court officer or government employee. The only exception to that would be in the context of where a local crime involves some federal issue (*e.g.*, violation of a federal civil rights law), in which instance a federal prosecutor for that area may decide to prosecute for the federal violation.

First Court Appearance

Early in the course of a criminal proceeding, the defendant will be brought into court and the charges brought against him or her by the government will be formally read. The defendant will be asked by the court whether he or she pleads guilty or not guilty to the charges. At that stage of the proceeding, the defendant is expected to have an attorney unless he or she has waived his or her right to have an attorney. If the defendant cannot afford to have an attorney and meets the local guidelines for the appointment of counsel, then the court will appoint an attorney to represent him or her in that criminal case.

Pleas

At any point during this process the defendant may plead guilty to the charge leveled against him or her. Likewise, at any stage during the process, the defendant or his or her attorney may conduct negotiations with the prosecutor to determine whether a plea to some lesser charge may be agreeable to the government. If such an agreement is reached, the plea agreement is brought to the attention of the court and the prosecution is concluded. The only thing left to be done is the imposition of whatever sentence has either been agreed to and accepted by the court or is otherwise established by the court. The judge has final control over what sentence is imposed regardless of what agreement the lawyers may have reached.

It's the Law

The judge has final control over what sentence is imposed.

Pretrial Proceedings

In most criminal prosecutions, the defendant has the right to appear at a *preliminary hearing* where some or all of the prosecution witnesses will be called for the purpose of presenting evidence to determine whether there is probable cause to support the arrest made by the police. This hearing is normally presided over by a judge or magistrate. The sole issue for determination at this preliminary hearing is whether probable cause exists. If probable cause is found to exist, then the next stage in the proceeding is presentation of the case to a grand jury.

A *grand jury* is a group of citizens who are convened by the court for the purpose of reviewing criminal cases as presented to them by the prosecutor. They determine again whether there is probable cause to believe that the defendant committed the crime with which he or she is charged. The grand jury can choose to indict the defendant for that criminal offense or can choose not to indict. Grand juries are frequently referred to as being rubber stamps of the prosecutor's office. The grand jury, although it is composed of unbiased citizens, only hears one side of the story. The evidence that is presented at a grand jury is chosen by the prosecutor. It normally comes through the testimony of police officers. The grand jurors do not hear from the defendant and do not hear the other side of the story. As one might expect, grand juries typically accept the recommendation of the prosecutor and indict the defendant for the crime charged.

Felonies and Misdemeanors

Criminal offenses can be divided into two general categories—felonies and misdemeanors. A *felony* is a crime for which a person can be imprisoned for more than a year. A *misdemeanor* is an offense for which a person can be imprisoned for up to a year. The criminal process regarding misdemeanors may differ dramatically from the criminal process as it applies to felonies. The defendant charged with a felony is entitled to greater protections and as such the procedure in regard to a felony case may be considerably more prolonged than that involving a misdemeanor. It is not at all unusual that for a misdemeanor charge the defendant simply appears in court on one occasion, and after being advised of his or her right to have an attorney, the case is tried on that one occasion. A felony charge may result, however, in several court appearances—first a hearing in regard to the setting of bond, then an arraignment, then a preliminary hearing, then an appearance for the setting of a trial date, then the appearance for any pretrial motions, and then, finally, the appearance for trial.

Traffic Court Cases

There is a third category of criminal offenses called *petty offenses.* Most of the crimes that fall into this category are traffic related, such as speeding, and are handled by the traffic court.

Traffic offenses, although not normally thought of as such, really are criminal offenses because they involve a potential criminal penalty. That criminal penalty may consist simply of a monetary fine or there may be actual arrest and imprisonment for more serious traffic offenses.

In most jurisdictions traffic offenses are handled in a very perfunctory fashion with a single judge hearing perhaps hundreds of cases in the course of a few hours. In most instances, these cases are presented by a police officer who simply stands before the judge and tells the judge what he or she saw or determined based upon his or her investigation. If there are witnesses involved, then those witnesses may be called to briefly explain what happened. The defendant is then given an opportunity to explain what happened if he or she wishes. The defendant, however, has no obligation to testify since his or her Fifth Amendment right against self-incrimination would apply in this proceeding.

If you have ever been to traffic court, you probably recall seeing a multitude of police officers in the courtroom. Those police officers are there to testify in cases in which they have issued tickets or made arrests. If, for some reason, the officer issuing the ticket does not show up for the traffic court date, then the case may be dismissed for lack of prosecution by the government. Likewise, if there was a witness to the traffic offense and the witness is the only one who can establish the government's case, the case may be dismissed if that witness does not show up for the traffic hearing. You may recall that the burden rests with the government to prove its case in a criminal prosecution. That burden applies in a traffic case. The government must present independent evidence either from a police officer or a witness to establish what happened. If the government cannot do that, then the government cannot meet its burden of proof and therefore the charge will be dismissed without the defendant ever having testified.

In some jurisdictions, traffic court cases are handled administratively and are presided over by an administrative hearing officer. An *administrative hearing officer* is a type of quasi-judge who has some of the authority of a judge but does not necessarily have that title or wear a robe in the hearing room.

Discovery

In some criminal prosecutions, pretrial *discovery* may be allowed. The *discovery* that is allowed in a criminal case is considerably more limited than what is allowed in a civil case. In a civil case, the prevailing philosophy is that a full disclosure of the facts and full discovery of the strong points and weak points of the other party's case is desirable in order to allow the parties to make an intelligent decision as to whether the case should be settled and, if so, how much it should be settled for. In the area of criminal law, the prevailing philosophy is that too much discovery is not a good thing because the information gathered by the defendant could conceivably be used to intimidate witnesses and to otherwise bog down the criminal justice system. As such, the amount of discovery allowed in a criminal case is typically limited compared to what is allowed in a civil case.

It's the Law
The amount of discovery allowed in a criminal case is typically limited.

Privilege

A privilege that exists in the criminal context is the privilege against *self-incrimination*. Within the Fifth Amendment it is stated that a person cannot be forced to be a witness against him- or herself. Simply put, a person who is a potential suspect in a criminal investigation cannot be forced to testify against him- or herself.

Jury Trial

Under the Sixth Amendment to the Constitution, a defendant in a criminal case has the right to a *jury trial*. That right to a jury trial is not unlimited—it may not apply to *petty offenses*. An offense may be characterized as petty if it carries a penalty of potential imprisonment of less than six months. Many states have expanded that right and grant jury trials for any offense that carries potential imprisonment. The right to a jury trial in some states applies to both sides. In other words, not only does the defendant have the right to request a jury trial but the government also has the right to request a jury trial.

The jury in a criminal case in most jurisdictions consists of twelve people. In most jurisdictions, the jury verdict must be unanimous.

The stages of a jury trial in a criminal case are much the same as those previously described in a civil case. Each side has the right to conduct *voir dire* of the jury in order to determine whether there are any members of the potential jury that may have any bias or predisposition about the case. Once a jury has been selected, the prosecution has the right to make an opening statement, followed by the defendant's opening statement. Then the government begins its presentation of evidence. At the conclusion of the government's case, the defendant has a right to make a motion to dismiss the government's case on the grounds of it being insufficient to justify conviction. Typically, that motion is denied by the court and then the defendant has the right to present his or her evidence.

A distinguishing characteristic of a criminal trial is that the government may not call the defendant to the witness stand. The defendant has an absolute right to be free of self-incrimination. Only the defendant can make the decision as to whether he or she testifies. Once the defendant chooses to testify, then he or she is subject to cross-examination by the prosecutor.

The Press

Some criminal cases attract a good deal of press coverage. If the press coverage has been so intensive that the local pool of potential jurors has been influenced, it is conceivable that the case could be moved from that jurisdiction to another locale where the press coverage has not been as intense. The press cannot be excluded from a criminal proceeding involving an adult. The Sixth Amendment to the Constitution guarantees the accused the right to a public trial, and the First Amendment guarantees the right of the public and the press to attend criminal trials. However, most courts in the U.S. do restrict the use of cameras in the courtroom. This is generally considered to be a means of controlling conduct in the courtroom and is not necessarily intended to restrict the right of the press to be present.

Aspects That Level the Playing Field

A trial, whether a civil case or a criminal case, is designed to be a truth seeking activity. The truth seeking capability of a trial on the civil side is frequently somewhat affected by the disparity in ability between lawyers. Similar disparities can apply in regard to a criminal case, but there are some aspects of a criminal case that are designed to level the playing field between the government and the defense. A prosecutor who is aware of information that is considered to be *exculpatory*—that would tend to show that the defendant is not guilty—must disclose that information to the defense prior to trial. The rationale behind that rule is based upon the truth seeking function of a trial.

A criminal trial is not simply a matter of gamesmanship, but a matter of getting all of the pertinent facts out before the jury and then letting the jury decide whether the defendant is guilty or not guilty. During the course of the trial, a prosecutor is somewhat restricted in the vehemence of his or her arguments to the jury. A prosecutor is subject to the general due process prohibition against prejudicial and inflammatory remarks to the jury.

Right of Confrontation

A defendant in any criminal case has the right to confront his or her accusers. This *right of confrontation* means that the defendant has an absolute right to be present at trial. If the defendant engages in outrageous behavior, then he or she can be restrained or placed in a separate room where he or she can see and hear the proceedings but not disrupt them. That, however, is a rather extraordinary measure in a criminal case.

That right of confrontation also means that the defense has a rather broad right as far as cross-examining those witnesses who testify against the defendant. In addition, that right of confrontation restricts the right of the government to put in evidence statements of persons who do not testify at trial. Such statements generally would be classified as hearsay and therefore would not be admissible. In a criminal case those hearsay statements further become objectionable because they may violate the defendant's right to confront his or her accusers.

Standard of Proof

The *standard of proof* in a criminal case is what is referred to as proof beyond a reasonable doubt. Proof *beyond a reasonable doubt* is a higher standard than either preponderance of the evidence or the clear and convincing standard. (See Chapter 5.) Proof beyond a reasonable doubt does not mean that the jury has to be absolutely certain of the defendant's guilt, but if a juror has a *reasonable doubt* as to whether the defendant is guilty then that juror should vote not guilty. Since a unanimous verdict is required in most jurisdictions in a criminal case, one juror with reasonable doubt can hang up a jury and prevent the government from getting a conviction. If the jury deliberations result in an eleven to one vote in favor of conviction (guilty), then typically the trial court will, on motion of the government, declare a mistrial and thereby allow the government to re-try the case.

Sentencing

The final stage of a criminal case in the trial court is sentencing. The federal judiciary as well as many states now operate under *sentencing guidelines.* These sentencing guidelines are very detailed and very complex formulas that govern the parameters of a sentence that a judge can impose on a defendant for a specific crime. Within those sentencing guidelines there are a variety of factors that may be considered by the court including but not limited to:

- ◆ the defendant's prior criminal history;
- ◆ the defendant's cooperation with the government in the investigation of other related crimes;
- ◆ the defendant's feelings of remorse after conviction; and,
- ◆ the nature and seriousness of the offense itself.

The purpose of these sentencing guidelines is to eliminate the significant disparity that can exist from one judge to another in sentences for the same crime.

The judiciary, to some extent, has been rather critical of sentencing guidelines because they significantly restrict a judge's discretion. The guidelines, however, do allow for exceptional circumstances when the sentence imposed may vary from what the guidelines call for. The purpose of the guidelines is admirable—to eliminate unfairness or gross disparity in the way that defendants are treated for similar crimes. But like any guidelines, they are not perfect.

Appeal

After a sentence has been imposed, the defendant has the right to pursue an *appeal.* All states now provide for appellate review. The availability of that appellate review cannot be conditioned upon the convicted defendant's financial status. If a trial transcript of the proceedings is required in order to pursue an appeal, then the government must provide that transcript for the indigent defendant. Likewise, the state must provide counsel for an appeal to an indigent defendant.

It's the Law
Once a defendant has been found not guilty, the government has no right to appeal that finding.

Once a defendant has been found not guilty, the government has no right to appeal that finding. The logic of this rule is that to allow appeals by the government would essentially allow the government to potentially utilize its vast resources to wear down the defendant.

Double Jeopardy

The *double jeopardy* clause of the Fifth Amendment provides that no person shall be tried twice for the same offense. Jeopardy is deemed to attach in jury trials once the jury is impaneled and sworn. The double jeopardy prohibition, however, is somewhat flexible. That is, if a mistrial is declared before a verdict is reached due to the inability of a jury to reach a unanimous verdict or for some reason other than misconduct on the part of the prosecution, then a new trial would not be deemed to be a violation of the double jeopardy clause. Double jeopardy also only applies to the governmental entity who is bringing the charge. (Recall the example involving Rodney King from p.13.)

Habeas Corpus

After sentencing and after all appeals have been exhausted, a criminal defendant may pursue another avenue in order to have his or her case reviewed. That avenue is what is referred to as a *habeas corpus* petition. The term *habeas corpus* literally means "you have the body." A *habeas corpus* petition is one requesting that the court compel the government to justify or explain what may appear to be some irregularity in the prosecution of that defendant. That is, a defendant who has been tried in state court and found guilty may appeal that conviction up through the state court system, through the intermediate court of appeals, if one exists in that state, and then to the high court of that state.

After having exhausted those appeals, he or she may file a petition for *habeas corpus* in federal court requesting that the federal judge direct the state authorities to show why this defendant should not be released from incarceration because of what may be deemed to be some irregularity in that state court prosecution.

Habeas corpus petitions were much more common years ago, as the courts more recently have somewhat restricted the rights of defendants to pursue that type of relief.

Criminal Justice in the Federal Court System

The procedure by which a criminal case is handled in the federal court is not dramatically different than that described above for the state courts. Within the federal court system, there is a specific set of rules called the Federal Rules of Criminal Procedure that governs the conduct of a criminal case. Within the federal system, the law enforcement agency initiating the prosecution is a federal law enforcement agency such as the FBI, Secret Service, or other federal agency rather than a local police department. Cases in federal court will be prosecuted by the U.S. Attorney's office that operates within that federal district. Crimes that are committed within that federal district will be tried in the U.S. District Court that has jurisdiction for that federal district, and will be subject to appeal to the Circuit Court of Appeals that covers that federal district.

One of the distinguishing features of the federal courts is that they are courts of limited jurisdiction. However, Congress over the last several years has enacted federal criminal statutes dealing with such things as carjacking and nonpayment of child support. Those traditionally have been offenses that would have been governed exclusively by state law and prosecuted exclusively in state court. Because Congress has passed federal legislation dealing with those issues, they may now also be prosecuted in federal court. The expanding criminal jurisdiction of the federal courts has been slow moving but fairly steady over the last several years. Our founding fathers would probably say that this ever-expanding scope of federal legislation is contrary to their intent.

Chapter Seven

Criminal Law and Specific Crimes

The distinguishing feature of criminal law is the element of punishment. The purpose of criminal law is to punish wrongdoers. If someone is accused of a crime and subsequently convicted of that crime, then they are to be punished. That is dramatically different than the purpose of civil law. Generally, civil law is intended to compensate someone for an injury suffered or to undo a wrong that has been committed. In the field of criminal law, the victim is not necessarily compensated, but the perpetrator is punished. In the eyes of the criminal justice system, the purpose of that punishment is to help reform the perpetrator; to restrain future misconduct by that perpetrator; to create a system of deterrents to other potential perpetrators; and, finally, to obtain retribution for the crime that has been committed.

Although most criminal prosecutions are initiated against individuals, there are certain types of crimes for which corporate entities may be responsible. Those crimes fall under the category of financial crimes—fraud and other types of financial transactions.

The ultimate punishment allowed in our criminal justice system is that of *capital punishment*. That form of punishment is reserved for the most heinous crimes.

Murder

At the heart of mystery novels is homicide, sometimes referred to as murder. There are different degrees of murder. The premeditated, willful, and deliberate killing of another is *murder one* or *capital murder*.

In most jurisdictions, the person who kills while attempting to inflict serious bodily injury on another has shown sufficient malice to be guilty of murder. In those jurisdictions where murder is divided into different degrees, this type of murder is generally referred to as *murder in the second degree*. What principally distinguishes murder in the first degree from murder in the second degree is the premeditation that is part of the murder one offense.

Example: *If Tony sets out to kill you, and then in fact does kill you (still with the intent to kill you), then that constitutes murder in the first degree. If, on the other hand, Tony kills you in the heat of an argument and there is no element of premeditation, then that may qualify as murder in the second degree. If Tony is simply negligent and as a result of that negligence you are killed, it may be negligent homicide.*

Felony murder arises where any death results during the commission of a felony. A felony is a crime for which a person can be imprisoned for more than a year. A misdemeanor is a crime for which a person can be imprisoned for up to a year. Many jurisdictions make distinctions as to whether felony murder will be murder one or murder two depending upon the type of felony that is being committed.

A rule that applies in many jurisdictions is the so-called *year and a day rule*. Under this rule, a death cannot be attributed to the defendant's wrongful conduct unless the death occurs within a year and a day of that conduct. So if the person died after a year and a day of the wrongful conduct, then the defendant could not be charged with murder.

Personal Crimes and Victimless Crimes

Murder is the most significant crime against a person. Other crimes against a person are such crimes as battery, assault, mayhem, forcible rape, kidnapping, and robbery. *Kidnapping* is the unlawful carrying away of a person typically for purposes of obtaining a ransom. *Robbery* is the theft of property from the control of another. It is to be distinguished from *burglary*, which involves an unlawful entry into a premises for the purpose of obtaining property or committing some other crime. *Rape* is forcible sexual intercourse with another.

In addition to these personal crimes, there are a number of so-called *victimless* crimes. Some people take issue with the use of the term *victimless* on the notion that all crimes involve a victim, whether it be the perpetrator or someone else. The crimes of prostitution, drug abuse, and obscenity are sometimes called victimless crimes.

Property Crimes

There also several crimes that are classified as crimes against property. *Larceny* is a property crime that involves the taking and carrying away of the valuable personal property of another with the intent to permanently deprive the person of that property. Larceny differs from *robbery* in that the property is not under the immediate control of the victim.

Example: *If Barbara walks into a department store and picks up a coat off the rack and walks out the door with the intent of not paying for the coat, then she has committed larceny. If, on the other hand, she snatches the coat out of Sally's hands on the street and runs off with it, she has committed a robbery.*

Embezzlement is a property crime that is defined as the fraudulent conversion of the property of another by a person who has lawful possession of the property. If an employee removes money from the cash drawer and converts that money to his or her own personal use, then that person has committed embezzlement. Embezzlement normally involves someone who is in a position of trust and has access to the money or property of another.

False pretenses is also a property crime. False pretenses is defined as obtaining title to property by knowingly or recklessly making a false representation of a presently existing fact of monetary significance that is intended to and does defraud the victim. False pretenses is very much like the civil claim of fraud.

Forgery is another property crime. The most common instruments involved in forgery are checks. If you have insufficient funds in your banking account and write a check on that bank account, it is not forgery. The check is genuine. Forgery is the false making or altering of a legally significant instrument (for instance, a check) with the intent to defraud.

Uttering is related to forgery. Uttering consists of negotiating or attempting to negotiate an instrument that is known to be false. This is very similar to simply passing a bad check. If you write a check on your own account when you know that there are not sufficient funds in the account, that, however, is not uttering but simply passing a bad check. The term uttering comes from the fact that words are uttered in presenting that document for negotiation.

Receiving stolen goods is another property crime. To be guilty of receiving stolen goods, the receiver must know or believe the goods were stolen.

Extortion is a property crime that involves making threats for the purpose of obtaining money or property. If someone threatens to expose you as a philanderer unless you give him or her $1,000, that may be extortion.

Burglary is another property crime. Burglary is breaking and entering the structure of another with the intent of committing a crime. Normally the crime that is intended to be committed is theft or larceny—removing something from the premises.

There are a multitude of other property crimes.

Intent

An essential element of a criminal offense is what is known as *mens rea* or *intent*. Different crimes may require different levels of intent. There are a variety of different ways that the courts have addressed these levels of intent. Two common distinctions, though somewhat confusing, are specific intent and general intent. A *specific intent* crime is one that calls for a particular state of mind in order to satisfy the elements of that offense.

> ## It's the Law
> *Different crimes may require different levels of intent.*

For instance, in first degree murder there must be premeditation—a specific intent to kill. In second degree murder, however, there need not be a specific intent to kill. There may simply be a *general intent*. If a person fires a gun into a crowd of strangers, with no intent to kill anyone, he or she could be guilty of second degree murder for acting recklessly.

Another aspect of intent is what is referred to as *transferred intent*. Transferred intent arises when a person intends to harm one victim but in fact harms another.

Example: *If Bobby throws a rock at you and rather than hitting you, hits your next door neighbor, he may still be guilty of the crime of assault and battery even though he did not intend to hit your neighbor. His intent is deemed to be transferred from you to the neighbor.*

Strict Liability and Vicarious Liability

In the chapter on tort law, strict liability and vicarious liability are discussed. To some extent, those concepts are also recognized in criminal law. *Strict liability* arises when a conviction can be obtained merely upon proof that the defendant perpetrated an act forbidden by statute. A common type of strict liability offense is a traffic violation. If you run a stop sign, it makes no difference what your intent was. The mere act of running the stop sign makes you guilty of a violation.

Vicarious liability can arise in the criminal context when the conduct of another person can be attributed to you.

Example: *If Debbie runs a restaurant and an employee of hers sells alcohol to a minor, then she may be liable under the local liquor laws.*

Actus Reus

Aside from intent, another essential element of most criminal violations is that of *actus reus*, meaning the guilty act. If a person merely forms the intent to kill someone, but never does anything to actually implement it, then he or she has not committed any crime. If, however, that person forms the intent, goes out and purchases the weapon, and enters into a conspiracy to use that weapon to kill someone, then he or she may be guilty of a crime. In order to constitute *actus reus*, the act must be voluntary.

These two critical elements of *mens rea* and *actus reus* must occur concurrently.

Example: *If Mark intentionally shoots to kill you, but misses and later accidentally kills you, he is not guilty of murder. At the time that Mark committed the act (**actus reus**) of accidentally killing you, he no longer had the intent (**mens rea**) of actually killing you.*

Attempted Crime

The mere attempt to commit a crime may also be a crime. An attempt to commit a crime normally involves a specific intent. For instance, attempted murder involves the specific intent to kill. If someone's intent, however, is only to cause serious bodily harm, then he or she cannot be guilty of attempted murder. Because attempt requires a specific intent, it is impossible to attempt a crime that by definition cannot be committed intentionally. For example, involuntary manslaughter cannot be attempted because it requires the wrongdoer to cause death *unintentionally*.

Solicitation

Another type of criminal behavior is *solicitation*. Solicitation involves a specific intent to engage in a particular type of criminal conduct. If I offer to pay you $50,000 to kill my business partner, that constitutes solicitation.

Accessories

The law also recognizes *principals* and *accessories* in criminal activity. The getaway man (driver) in a bank robbery who does not actually go into the bank is an accessory. That person probably will be punished in a similar way as the principals, who were actually in the bank. If, however, a person not even at the scene of the bank robbery assists the bank robbers in getting the getaway vehicle, knowing that it was to be used for that purpose, then he or she also may be an accessory. An accessory in that context probably would not be subject to the same punishment as a principal.

A person could also become an accessory by assisting the bank robbers in eluding the police. In that event, he or she would be an *accessory after the fact*. Again, in that type of circumstance, he or she probably would not be subject to the same punishment as the principals.

More difficult cases arise when a person is present at the time of a crime under circumstances that suggest approval. Normally, this is not sufficient to convict a person of a criminal violation. One exception to this would be an instance in which the defendant is under a duty to act.

Example: *If a father stands by idly while his minor son attacks a third person, he could—at least in some states—be guilty of a criminal violation.*

Conspiracy

Prosecutors over the last several years have become more daring in bringing conspiracy charges against persons involved in criminal behavior. *Conspiracy* is an agreement between two or more persons to commit an unlawful act or to commit a lawful act in an unlawful manner, when one or more persons commit an overt act in furtherance of the conspiracy. In a conspiracy case, the agreement itself is the *actus reus* and the intent to commit the unlawful act is the *mens rea*.

Suppose you and I agree to rob a bank. The agreement alone does not constitute a conspiracy. If, however, I go out and buy a handgun that is to be used in the robbery, at that point I have committed an overt act to pursue the conspiracy and at that point I may be guilty of the crime of conspiracy.

Defenses

There are several defenses that can be raised in a criminal case.

Insanity

One of the more newsworthy defenses is that of *insanity*. Different states have adopted different rules as to how insanity is to be determined.

Some states adopt a simple test known as the *M'Naghten rule*, which is simply a determination of whether the perpetrator was able to distinguish right from wrong. Other states adopt the *irresistible impulse* test that may apply when a defendant knew he or she was doing wrong, but the status of his or her mind prevented him or her from controlling his or her conduct—he or she was overtaken by an irresistible impulse to engage in that behavior.

The District of Columbia adopted the *Durham test* several years ago. It provides that an accused is not criminally responsible if his or her unlawful act was the product of mental disease or mental defect. These types of insanity defenses are generally the subject of a good deal of controversy and normally involve expert testimony from psychiatrists or other mental health professionals.

Intoxication

Another defense that can be raised is *intoxication*. If a crime requires specific intent, then a person who is intoxicated may be incapable of forming that specific intent.

Coercion

Coercion arises when there is duress. The bank teller who turns over the bank's money to the robber is acting under duress and therefore is not guilty of larceny in removing the money from the drawer. He or she is coerced in releasing the money.

Necessity

A woman who is threatened with sexual assault, and who then breaks down a neighbor's front door to seek refuge is not guilty of burglary because her conduct is governed by the defense of *necessity*. She needed to find safety.

It's the Law

The purpose of the entrapment defense is to prevent the government from manufacturing a crime.

Entrapment

Entrapment is a much more difficult defense. The purpose of the entrapment defense is to prevent the government from manufacturing a crime. An undercover police officer who offers to purchase narcotics from someone who he or she believes to be a pusher is not guilty of entrapment. However, an undercover police officer who applies immense pressure to a suspect to sell him or her narcotics by establishing a friendship with him or her and then playing on that friendship to overcome that person's unwillingness to sell narcotics probably would be guilty of entrapment.

Vagueness

Another defense that may be raised to some criminal violations is that of *vagueness*. The U.S. Constitution precludes punishing a person under a statute that is too vague to be understood. A statute should be sufficiently clear that a reasonable person could determine what conduct is forbidden, and the statute should be sufficiently clear as to prevent arbitrary enforcement by the police. *Loitering* statutes over the years have been subject to tests for vagueness. For example, if they preclude any person from being on a public street at any time, then they may be subject to constitutional challenges for vagueness.

Self-Defense

The ultimate defense to a crime against a person is *self-defense*. As a general rule, a person may use whatever force is reasonably necessary to prevent immediate and unlawful harm to him- or herself. Some jurisdictions have adopted the *retreat rule* that requires a person who can safely retreat to do so before using deadly force.

In general, the defense of self-defense permits a person to employ reasonable, nondeadly force to resist an unlawful arrest. However, as a practical matter, resisting an unlawful arrest is a risky maneuver because it could result in worse physical harm to the accused.

Protection of Property

A related defense in property crimes is *protection of property.* As a general rule, a person can use whatever force, short of deadly force, that reasonably appears to be necessary to protect property. A classic case in that regard involved the homeowner who laid a trap in his home consisting of a spring gun that fired when the burglar entered the front door. Since a spring gun automatically fires, anyone entering the house is at risk. And since human life is valued over property, the homeowner cannot claim defense of property when someone was killed entering the house.

Chapter Eight

Juvenile Law

Juvenile Court is sometimes referred to by lawyers and law enforcement officers as *Kiddie Court*. The Juvenile Court in some jurisdictions, however, can be more than simply what the name may imply. In some jurisdictions, it may actually be a type of Family Court wherein all different types of family disputes may be resolved. This chapter will not deal with family law issues (see Chapter 14), it will simply deal with issues of juvenile justice.

It's the Law
A juvenile arrested and processed through the juvenile court system does not have to report that offense on a job application.

The logic behind the juvenile court system in the United States is that because juveniles are under-age, they should be dealt with in a different fashion than adults. In many jurisdictions, juvenile offenses are not even referred to as criminal offenses. Juvenile records in most jurisdictions are strictly confidential and are not subject to public access either by means of *subpoena* or other inquiry. As such, a juvenile arrested and processed through the Juvenile Court does not have to report that offense on a job application or other type of inquiry unless directly asked about it since the inquiry itself is not going to be subject to any public confirmation.

Proceedings in Juvenile Court are all conducted by a judge with no jury present. For certain types of offenses, however, a juvenile may be transferred to the adult system and may be tried as an adult with all the consequences that might apply to an adult. (That type of treatment is generally reserved for more serious offenses.)

An offense in Juvenile Court is generally handled in a somewhat informal fashion. There may be a prosecutor present in Juvenile Court. That prosecutor represents the interest of the government or the victim. The prosecutor may present evidence in front of the judge who then hears from the defense and renders a decision. That decision normally consists of a finding of whether the juvenile is *involved*. If so there may be some punishment imposed. That punishment may consist simply of a monetary fine, performing some community service, or for more extreme circumstances, confinement to a juvenile home for a period of time.

The thrust of the juvenile court system is to be instructive and rehabilitative—to instruct the juvenile as to the error of his or her ways and to assist him or her with rehabilitation. That is dramatically different from the thrust of the adult court system, which may have an element of rehabilitation about it, but is more oriented toward a finding of guilt or innocence and then punishing the guilty.

Teen Rights

Teenagers who are under age 18 are citizens, and therefore—at least theoretically—have many of the same rights as adult citizens. However, in most states, minors are considered to be legally incompetent, which means they cannot enter into contractual relationships and, in large measure, are subject to the control of parents. However, that does not mean their rights can be trampled. For instance, in regard to school-related activities, juveniles do have certain due process rights in terms of being informed of any charges that are made against them and having a right to confront those charges through some sort of hearing process. The U.S. Supreme Court has stated that the schools do have a great deal of latitude in terms of maintaining proper discipline and decorum on school property. Therefore, privacy rights that may apply to people in their own home do not necessarily apply in a public school.

Example: If a student is hoarding drugs in his locker, he probably
        does not have a privacy right to that locker. The locker is
        not his property—it is public property, and he is violating
        the law by storing drugs in that locker. Therefore, if the
        school officials decide to go into that locker without his
        consent, they can do so.

Following up on that same example, suppose that a teacher
accuses a student of hoarding drugs in his locker but there is no
direct proof of that. Is it appropriate to put a memorandum in the
student's file stating that accusation? It probably would not be
appropriate to do so and at the very least the student would have
the right to certain procedural due process rights consisting of the
right to know what the charge is that is being made against him
and then the right to be heard on that charge. In this particular
example, the student would have a right to know what the content is of that accusation from the teacher and then would have
a right to make a presentation in front of the principal or other
appropriate school official as to why that allegation is not true.

Driver's License

Teenagers are all interested in acquiring a driver's license. Many
of them operate under the misperception that they have a right
to a driver's license. No one has a right to a driver's license. The
possession of a driver's license is a privilege. It can be taken away
from any holder by the state based upon infractions. In the case
of juveniles, most states impose more stringent requirements in
terms of taking a driver education course and operating under
the supervision of an adult driver for a period of time before that
person can actually get a driver's license. Once the driver's license
is issued, there is typically a probationary-type period in which
the license can be taken away from that juvenile for any serious
infraction. In that regard, juveniles are treated somewhat differ-
ently than adults.

Parental Responsibility

Most states are concerned about responsibility of parents for the actions of their children. Many states have enacted laws imposing liability upon the parents for misconduct of their children resulting in property damage. For instance, if your juvenile eggs the next door neighbor's home, resulting in property damage, you may be liable for that damage as a parent. However, the states that have enacted such laws typically put a cap on the extent of the parental liability in terms of dollars.

Chapter Nine

What to Expect if Called as a Juror

As citizens, we all have an obligation to serve as jurors when summoned. Your summons to appear as a juror may come from a state court or from a federal court. Jurors are chosen by different means in different jurisdictions. Some jurisdictions draw from records of the Department of Motor Vehicles, property owner records, and voting records. Other jurisdictions may draw from only one or two of these things.

Lawyers and judges have debated the merits of how jurors should be chosen for many years. Most judges probably think that jurors should be drawn from voting lists and also from property ownership rolls because that tends to produce a group of potential jurors that are more involved in the community. People that are simply listed with the Department of Motor Vehicles as being licensed drivers but who are not voters or property owners may be less involved in their community. The merits of the respective positions on that issue lie in the eyes of the beholder.

In any event, if you are called as a juror, you must respond unless you are subject to one of the exemptions that applies in your jurisdiction. Over the last several years, the number of exemptions that have applied has been narrowed in most states. It used to be that the exemptions were so broad that the court frequently was left with the only eligible jurors being housewives. That is not in any way to diminish the ability of housewives to decide the merits of litigation, but the goal of a jury trial is to provide a trial by one's peers. That is not accomplished if the jury is limited to a narrow segment of the community.

When you are called as a juror, you will have the opportunity to state any particular problems you may have with serving. In most instances, however, unless the reason you cannot serve is extremely compelling and virtually of an emergency nature, then your excuse for not serving will likely be rejected by the court.

Your initial selection for service in a courtroom is a matter of a random draw. A certain number of jurors will be sent to a particular courtroom assigned to a judge who has been assigned a particular case. Once you are sent to that courtroom, you may be asked certain preliminary questions that are designed to determine whether there is something that would automatically disqualify you from jury service. Then the lawyers (or, in some cases, the judge) will have the opportunity to conduct what is called *voir dire*, a questioning process to determine whether you have any particular bias or interest in the outcome of the case. If you do, you may be dismissed from service for that reason. (See Chapter 5 for more specific information.)

If a case is going to last for several days, alternate jurors may be chosen. Typically, those alternate jurors will not be identified to the jury members themselves, since the knowledge that you were an alternate may affect the level of attention that you would apply to the case. Once all of the evidence is concluded and the closing arguments have been completed, the alternate jurors may be excused.

One thing that frequently comes up during the course of jury service is whether jurors are allowed to take notes or to ask questions during the proceeding. That is a matter of discretion of the individual judge and can vary dramatically from state to state and from courtroom to courtroom. Some judges allow jurors to take notes; others do not. Some judges allow jurors to ask questions, while others do not.

The logic behind the jury system is this: since the parties themselves are not able to resolve the particular dispute that has been brought to the courtroom, the best way to resolve the dispute is to have

It's the Law
Some judges allow jurors to take notes; others do not.

a group of unbiased citizens hear the evidence (in an objective fashion) and then decide that case fairly, based solely upon the evidence presented to them in the courtroom. Trial lawyers will tell you that the jury system is the great equalizer. The poorest citizen in this country can sue the mightiest corporation, and when those two parties come before a jury, they are equal. The jury is to treat each party with the same respect and attention.

The proponents of tort reform maintain that the jury system is a system that has gone awry. They maintain that jurors frequently award outlandish sums for ridiculous cases. Although it is not unheard of that juries do sometimes *runaway*, that is very much the exception. Even if the jury does do something that is contrary to the evidence and the law as given to them, the trial judge always has the authority to correct that by reversing the jury verdict in a criminal case if the defendant was wrongfully convicted or in a civil case by reducing the amount of the verdict if it is too high.

Chapter Ten

What to Expect if Called as a Witness

Any party to a lawsuit or a criminal proceeding has the authority to subpoena witnesses. The power to subpoena witnesses is a basic constitutional right, since witnesses are the primary form by which evidence is presented. If parties could not present witnesses, then they could not present evidence in support of their case. The way a witness is compelled to appear in court is by means of a subpoena. The word *subpoena* literally means *under penalty.*

A subpoena is a court directive telling a person to appear at a particular place and time for the purposes of giving testimony. A subpoena may be for you to appear at a trial or at a deposition. (A *deposition* is a means of discovery conducted in most civil litigation, wherein the attorneys have the opportunity to ask witnesses what they know about a particular event relevant to that lawsuit.)

It's the Law

A subpoena is a court directive telling a person to appear at a particular place and time for the purposes of giving testimony.

If you should be served with a subpoena, the subpoena will typically indicate the name, address, and phone number of the attorney that requested you to appear. You should feel free to call that attorney and find out why you have been subpoenaed. If the date and time of the subpoena is not convenient for you, then you should inquire as to whether that date and time can be changed. If the attorney tells you that the date and time cannot be changed and you simply are not able to appear, then you need to bring that to the attention of the court immediately so the issue can be resolved by the court.

If you are subpoenaed to appear for trial or for a deposition, the local rules of the court may require that the attorney pay you a fee for your traveling expenses and for time that you lose from work. That is something that is governed by law and something that you should inquire about.

Sometimes witnesses ask whether they can ask questions during the course of the proceeding. Typically the answer to that question is no. You have been subpoenaed to give information and not to make inquiries on your own. That does not mean that during the course of a proceeding you may not stop and ask a question. If a *bona fide* question occurs to you, you should ask it. You may be told that your question cannot be answered or you may be provided with an appropriate answer.

The purpose of your appearing to testify is to respond to particular questions that are asked of you by the attorneys, the parties, or the court. Once that questioning has been completed, you will be excused and allowed to proceed with your normal routine. In some instances, after you have finished testifying, the judge may tell you that you have to remain in the courthouse because you may be called again as a witness. If that presents a problem for you, you need to bring that to the attention of the court immediately so that the issue can be dealt with. Most judges and attorneys are willing to work with witnesses in order to accommodate their schedules. The burden, however, is upon the witness to bring those issues to the attention of the court or the attorneys.

Chapter Eleven
Alternative Dispute Resolution

Alternative Dispute Resolution (ADR) has become extremely popular in the last ten to twenty years. Alternative Dispute Resolution is a mechanism by which civil disputes are resolved as an alternative to civil litigation.

Alternative Dispute Resolution, in some instances, may be mandatory and in other instances it is voluntary.

Mandatory Alternative Dispute Resolution is found in many forms of contracts such as brokerage contracts, employment contracts, and construction contracts. For instance, if you enter into a brokerage contract with a stock broker the contract is probably going to contain a mandatory arbitration clause that requires you to arbitrate any dispute that you may have with the broker as an alternative to filing suit against the broker.

In employment contracts, it is quite common for an employer to insert mandatory Alternative Dispute Resolutions such as arbitration or mediation as an alternative to filing suit.

The three different forms of Alternative Dispute Resolution are arbitration, neutral case evaluation, and mediation.

Arbitration is an alternative to a trial before a judge and/or jury. In most arbitrations there is one arbitrator who acts as the judge, although in some instances there may be more than one arbitrator who collectively act as the judge or judges to decide the case. Arbitrators act in all instances without a jury.

The arbitrator is normally picked by the parties. If the parties are not able to agree on who the arbitrator should be, then in most arbitration agreements there is a mechanism as to how the arbitrator will be chosen.

Arbitration as a means of Alternative Dispute Resolution may be preferred by some parties over a court trial because it is speedier and, in some cases, may be less expensive.

Most contracts with general contractors and architects have arbitration clauses in them. The individual consumer should be wary of mandatory arbitration provisions in any contract because it constitutes a waiver of the right to a jury trial. The consumer's right to a jury trial is a potent weapon to have in the event of a dispute arising with a contractor, architect, or other party to the contract.

The selling point that arbitration is less expensive than a court trial is not always the case. Most arbitrators are professionals who expect to be paid for their time. If you are involved in a multi-day arbitration hearing, then you may be looking at paying thousands of dollars in the form of arbitration fees in addition to paying your own attorney's fees. A trial in front of a judge generally only carries with it the expense of filing suit at the courthouse, which in most jurisdictions is only a couple hundred dollars.

One cost saving feature of arbitration is that there may be little or no discovery such as you see in civil litigation. Depending on the facts of your case, the lack of a discovery process may be an advantage to the consumer.

A disadvantage to arbitration is that most arbitrators are professionals in that particular field, *i.e.,* architects, engineers, brokers. Most of them are not trained in the law or in contract interpretation. Lawyers and judges are trained in the law and contract interpretation. In that sense, it may be more prudent to have a judge deciding your case as opposed to an arbitrator.

In addition, a judge is more likely than an arbitrator to be truly neutral in any dispute resolution process. Judges are required by law and professional ethics to be neutral.

In general, mandatory arbitration clauses in contracts are not to the advantage of the consumer. If that is an issue in a contract you are negotiating, then you should consider whether the arbitration clause can be made voluntary as opposed to mandatory.

Neutral case evaluation is another form of Alternative Dispute Resolution that is designed to provide some guidance to the parties as to how their dispute may be resolved. A neutral case evaluator may be from any profession but most often is a lawyer or a judge. In a neutral case evaluation the parties may submit written and/or oral presentations to the evaluator as to the merits of their case. The neutral case evaluator may then ask for further explanations on certain issues, and then the neutral case evaluator will render a non-binding recommendation as to what the case is worth or how it should be resolved. For example, in injury cases, the evaluator may come up with a dollar amount value as to what the case is worth. In domestic relations cases, the evaluator may come up with a means of resolving a custody dispute dealing with the children. Likewise, in a domestic relations dispute, the evaluator may come up with a formula by which the marital property is to be divided.

Whatever evaluation is reached by the neutral case evaluator, it is purely a recommendation which is intended to serve as a guide to the parties in evaluating the case and hopefully reaching a settlement.

The idea of settlement sometimes is a difficult concept for non-lawyers to deal with. In general, a settlement is preferable to a court imposed decision. A settlement implies that the parties have reached some agreement that each of them can live with. A court imposed decision or verdict frequently is one that neither party is going to be happy with. Some cases, however, simply cannot be settled and therefore have to be presented to a judge or jury for resolution.

Neutral case evaluation is frequently a follow-up to mediation. Mediation is conducted by a neutral mediator whose sole objective is to help the parties reach a settlement. *Mediation* is normally voluntary, *i.e.*, either party can decide not to settle.

The mediation process is purposely informal and may begin with an informal presentation by either party as to the merits of their case, followed up by the mediator talking with the parties either in front of each other or individually. The sole purpose of mediation is to see if the mediator can help the parties reach a settlement. A skillful mediator can provide a great deal of assistance in helping the parties bridge the gap between what one party may want and what the other party is willing to offer.

If the mediation process is not successful in reaching a settlement, then frequently it is followed by a neutral case evaluation wherein the mediator changes the hat that is being worn and provides a neutral case evaluation as to what the case may be worth.

Some state laws mandate ADR before certain civil suits may be filed. In particular, this is seen in regards to medical malpractice actions where some states require mediation or non-binding arbitration as a prelude to filing suit.

Section Three

Areas of the Law

Chapter Twelve

Contracts

Life is about agreements. The materials in this section explore these agreements.

Agreements you make with others are often called contracts, but there are several variations on this. You have employment contracts and marital contracts; your lease is a contract, as are arrangements with creditors.

The first two chapters of this section cover the laws of contracts and torts. This serves as an introduction to the remaining chapters that cover specific areas in which the principles of contract law and tort law are applied.

A *contract* is an agreement between two persons to either do something or not to do something in exchange for some form of consideration. An agreement may come in several different forms. The agreement may be *implied* as a result of the conduct of the parties. On the other hand, the agreement may be *expressed*, meaning that the parties have expressly stated what their intentions are and what they wish to obtain as a result of the agreement. An expressed contract may be in writing or it may be oral. Either type

It's the Law

A contract may be in writing or it may be oral.

of contract is equally enforceable in most instances, although a written contract is always preferable because it clearly sets forth the terms of the agreement. An oral contract is always subject to dispute, because the parties may have different recollections of exactly what they agreed to.

Sometimes people classify contracts as *unilateral* or *bilateral*. A *unilateral* contract might be most easily thought of as one in which the offer can be accepted only by doing some act. For instance, if your neighbor offers a $100 reward for the return of his cat, then you can accept that offer only by returning the cat.

A *bilateral* contract, on the other hand, is one where the giving of a promise is the expected consideration. Most contracts are bilateral. For example, you agree to buy my car for $100. You have agreed to do something (pay me $100) and I have agreed to do something (sell you my car).

Offer and Acceptance

The way that an agreement comes about is generally through an *offer* being made by one party and then that offer being *accepted* by the other party.

> **Example:** *If Joe were to send you a letter offering to paint your house for $100 with such work to be accomplished by a certain date and you then wrote on the bottom of the letter that these terms were agreeable and sent that back to Joe, that letter would constitute a written contract. The offer was in the form of the letter. The acceptance came in the form of your acknowledging the agreement. The consideration for the agreement is the $100 to be paid for the services rendered.*

The offer may come in two different forms—written or oral form. The more precise the terms of the offer, the better off the parties will be in establishing the certainty of their agreement. A common example of an offer is an advertisement that may appear in the newspaper by a car dealer offering to sell a used Toyota Camry for $17,500.

Suppose you were to see that advertisement and go to the dealership prepared to pay $17,500. If the dealer then told you that there were other terms that were not stated in the advertisement (handling charges, processing fees, and other such fees), you could rightfully tell the dealer that it made an offer to sell this vehicle for $17,500 and you are prepared to pay it. The dealer is obliged to sell the vehicle to you for that amount. (Of course on top of that $17,500 would be any taxes that are mandated by law.) The advertisement constituted an offer and you accepted the offer for the agreed upon consideration of $17,500.

If, on the other hand, you had come into the dealership and rather than offering $17,500, you offered to pay $17,000 for the vehicle, then that would be a *counteroffer*. A counteroffer is, by its very terms, a rejection of the original offer. The dealership would be free to reject your counteroffer.

There are several different ways that an offer may be framed. The person making the offer may state certain terms and conditions that have to be met in order for the offer to be accepted. If those terms and conditions are not met, then there cannot be a valid acceptance of the offer.

Consideration

Consideration is a very elusive but important concept. An easy way to think of it is as the *tit for tat*, the *quid pro quo*, or, to put it another way, it is simply the meat of the agreement. If there is no consideration, then there is no contract. Going back to the example of the house painting, if Joe wrote you a letter offering to paint your house but never stated when he would finish it or what compensation he expected and you simply wrote back saying that those terms were agreeable, that would probably not be a contract because there is no consideration stated.

Typically the performance of a preexisting legal duty cannot serve as consideration for a contract. For instance, if you are already under a duty to perform a certain act and you then promise to do it as the consideration for a contract, that consideration is insufficient.

Forbearance to do a certain act may serve as consideration.

Example: *If Connie agrees not to sue you for payment of $100, then that is sufficient consideration to make a contract enforceable. That forbearance serves as a legal detriment and therefore is sufficient consideration.*

Auctions

Most people have probably had the experience of attending an auction. The conduct of an auctioneer is similar to negotiating a contract. The auctioneer is putting a product on the market for sale and by announcing certain figures, he or she is requesting offers to purchase the item for that price. If you raise your hand and offer the number that the auctioneer has mentioned, then that is deemed to be an offer for the consideration as stated by the auctioneer. When the auctioneer drops the gavel on the highest offer, that is deemed to be an acceptance of that last offer. As part of any auction, there may also be certain published conditions that are made part of the auction. If that is so, then by bidding at the auction, you have agreed to those terms.

Uniform Commercial Code (UCC)

Contracts are the foundation upon which our economic system is built. They are of such importance that a body of law has developed known as the *Uniform Commercial Code*. This uniform law has been adopted by most states in the Union—either in whole or in part—and lays out certain principles dealing with commercial transactions (contracts). The Uniform Commercial Code, in large measure, governs the conduct between merchants and other parties dealing with merchants.

The Uniform Commercial Code establishes legal principles that control many business transactions. For instance, when you buy a piece of exercise equipment from a sporting goods store, your legal rights to return that equipment, to get replacement parts, or to file suit for a problem related to the equipment are all governed both by the warranty that comes with the product and also by the Uniform Commercial Code.

The Uniform Commercial Code also governs transactions involving security instruments and negotiable instruments. A *security instrument* is a document (typically filed at a courthouse or other public repository) that is designed to put the public on notice that a particular item of personal property, which may be found at a particular location, is security for a debt of the owner of that property to another person.

A security instrument in that regard is similar to a mortgage on your home. A mortgage is a type of security instrument that is designed to secure the mortgage lender in the event you do not make your monthly mortgage payments. If you fail to make your monthly mortgage payments, then the lender has the right to foreclose and to sell your property at public auction.

The Uniform Commercial Code also deals with negotiable instruments. A *negotiable instrument* is any instrument that may be negotiated or sold for value. For instance, a *promissory note* wherein one person promises to pay another a fixed amount of money is a negotiable instrument. Likewise, a check is a negotiable instrument. The Uniform Commercial Code deals with the law governing those types of instruments.

Statute of Frauds

Contracts may either be in writing or oral. Whether the contract is oral or in writing, it is equally valid, although there may be problems enforcing certain types of contracts that are not in writing. Most states have adopted, in some form or another, a law know as the *Statute of Frauds*. The Statute of Frauds is a law that is designed to minimize the possibility of fraudulent behavior in certain types of transactions. For instance, a person buying or selling land cannot enforce a contract of sale for land unless that contract is in writing. The logic behind that requirement is that over the years, there has been so much litigation relating to oral contracts for the sale of

It's the Law
The Statute of Frauds is designed to minimize the possibility of fraudulent behavior.

land and allegations of fraudulent behavior that those types of contracts must be in writing and be signed by the person against whom the agreement is being enforced. That type of requirement is designed to minimize the likelihood of there being any fraud perpetrated against the buyer. If the seller signs the agreement and agrees to sell the land for a certain price and all of that is confirmed in writing, then the chance of that transaction being fraudulent is considerably reduced.

Other types of transactions that typically need to be in writing to be enforceable are transactions that involve pledging the credit of another for a transaction, agreements to marry, agreements to pay real estate brokerage commissions, agreements that cannot be performed within one year, and agreements to lend money or extend credit for a significant amount, such as $25,000 or more. All of those types of transactions are ones that over the years have been found to be the subject of frequent litigation with allegations being made of fraud. Because of that, many states have found it best to require those types of transactions be put in writing and signed by the party against whom enforcement of the contract is being sought.

Defenses to Contracts

There are several defenses that can conceivably be asserted to a claim to enforce a contract. For instance, if one of the parties was a minor or suffering from mental incompetency at the time the contract was entered into, then those facts may be defenses to the validity of the contract. This defense is called *lack of capacity* to contract. Likewise, if there was a *mutual mistake* by the parties, then that could void a contract on the theory that there has been no meeting of the minds and therefore no agreement.

Example: A mutual mistake might arise in a circumstance in which the seller offers to sell his 1964 Cadillac that is parked in front of his home and the purchaser agrees to buy the 1964 Cadillac parked in front of the home. However, it turns out that there were in fact two 1964 Cadillacs parked in front of this home and the parties were referring to different vehicles when they entered into what they thought was their agreement. In that type of circumstance, there has been no meeting of the minds because the parties were mutually mistaken as to which vehicle was being sold.

It is not unheard of that in the course of defending a contract claim, the defendant may claim that he or she was induced to enter into the contract due to fraud on the part of the other party. *Fraud can be loosely defined as a misrepresentation of a material fact.*

Example: *You want to buy a house. You ask the sellers whether they have ever had a wet basement. The sellers tell you that they have never had a wet basement even though they know full well that it is untrue. That misrepresentation may constitute fraud.*

> *If you then proceed to buy the house, based upon the false representation, and find out after the sale that in fact the basement does leak, then you may sue the sellers for the fraud. To make your claim, you must have been induced to enter into the contract and you must have suffered certain damages. In this case, you bought a house that was faulty and, therefore, worth less than what you paid.*

Other conceivable defenses to a contract claim could come in the form of duress, undue influence, impossibility, and frustration. *Duress* is simply a threat or perceived threat to induce a party to enter into a contract. If someone puts a gun to your head and makes you sign a contract, that contract is not enforceable because you were operating under duress. Duress may also come in a number of other forms that may be considerably more subtle.

Undue influence arises when certain persons may have a great deal of control over a party and utilize that control in order to unduly influence a person to enter into a contract.

Example: *Betty holds a power of attorney for her next door neighbor, who is 94. The power of attorney authorizes Betty to conduct all of the financial affairs for her neighbor. If Betty encourages her next door neighbor to sign a contract selling his home for $100,000 under market value, that would be an example of undue influence. It would be a basis for setting aside that contract of sale.*

Impossibility arises where it truly becomes impossible to perform a contract due to something that is unforeseen by the parties. For

> ### It's the Law
> *Most contracts can and should be brief and straightforward.*

instance, the destruction of the World Trade Center made the performance of the leases for that building impossible. A related concept is that of *frustration of purpose*. For instance, during the inauguration of a new president, there may be certain contracts entered into. If the inauguration, however, is canceled, then the purpose of those contracts has been frustrated. If you were one of the suppliers who agreed to provide the grandstands for the inauguration, the U. S. Government may be able to void the contract with you since the inauguration is not going forward.

If you have ever read a multi-page contract drafted by an attorney, you probably found it to be a nightmarish experience. Although complicated business transactions call for contracts that are precise and complex, most contracts can and should be brief and straightforward. To the extent that there is any ambiguity in a contract, typically that ambiguity is interpreted against the party that drafted the contract.

Parol Evidence

Terms within the contract that are not expressly defined are typically given their dictionary definition by any court that may be called upon to interpret the contract. A rule of evidence that is important in regard to contract interpretation is the *parol evidence rule*. It declares that statements made by the parties prior to the signing of the contract will not be considered by a court in a contract dispute. The rule is well recognized and may be further strengthened by language within the contract itself that expressly says that the parties are only bound by the terms of the contract as set forth in the four corners of the document. The logic behind the parol evidence rule is that parties should not rely on precontract statements to define the intent of their agreement when, in fact, they have gone to the pains of putting their agreement in writing with the understanding that the writing constitutes the entire agreement.

The parol evidence rule may seem to be somewhat inconsistent with the example of how a party was fraudulently induced to enter into a contract for the sale of a home. The parol evidence rule, however, should not be confused with that instance of fraud. Fraudulent statements that are made to induce a party to enter into a contract are not deemed to be governed by the parol evidence rule. Fraudulent statements may be a basis for setting aside the contract because those fraudulent statements undermine the integrity and fairness of the agreement.

The meaning of a contract may also be garnered from looking at the prior course of dealing between the parties to this contract. That is, their prior course of dealing may give some clue as to what they intended the contract to mean.

Conditions to Performance

Once a contract has been entered into, the parties are obviously interested in the performance of the contract. It is not unusual, however, that there are certain conditions imposed on one or both parties before performance is necessary. For example, in your typical homeowners insurance contract, a condition that you must satisfy before your insurance company is obliged to make any payments to you is to provide a sworn proof of loss statement itemizing the damage that you are claiming. The insurance company also has the right to examine you under oath as to that claim. Once those conditions have been satisfied, the insurance company has an obligation to pay you for the damages incurred that are covered by your policy.

Sometimes those conditions within the contract may be the subject of what is referred to as *waiver* or *estoppel*. A condition may be *waived* if the insurance company informs you that you do not have to comply with that condition. A waiver is a relinquishment of a known right. If the insurance company has a right to require that you file a written proof of loss and they expressly waive that or tell you that you do not have to file a written proof of loss, then that constitutes a waiver of that condition.

In some instances, a party may be *estopped* from requesting that the conditions be satisfied. For instance, again referring to the insurance claim, if the insurance adjuster handling the matter told you that he would complete the proof of loss form and then submit it to you for your signature within the time allowed by the contract and you relied upon that representation, then the insurance carrier may be estopped from denying coverage to you for failing to have filed the proof of loss form within the time allowed.

An estoppel arises when a party makes a representation and the other party relies upon that representation to his or her detriment. In the example, the insurance adjuster represented that he would complete the proof of loss form. You relied upon that, and as a result of that adjuster's failure to do what he said he would do, your proof of loss form was not submitted in a timely fashion. In that circumstance, the insurance company would be estopped from denying your claim for failing to comply with the condition.

Payment of Attorney's Fees

Contracts are the foundation of our commercial system. A contract is an agreement. If the agreement is violated then the person who is in violation is liable for the damages called for under the contract. If Joe agrees to paint your house for $100 by a certain date, and after completing the job satisfactorily you refuse to pay Joe, then you are in breach of the contract and he can sue you for $100. If Joe has to hire an attorney to file that lawsuit, then he may be able to recover his attorney's fees *provided that the contract allows for that.*

The general rule of law in the United States is that each party has to pay its own attorney's fees regardless of who prevails. There has been a movement over the last several years to require that in civil litigation the losing party pay the attorney's fees of the winning party. This is the law in some countries. But the United States has never adopted that rule because it has been felt that such a rule would deter worthy litigants from bringing claims that are justifiable if they thought that there was any chance of their losing and thereby having to pay the attorney's fees of the opposing party.

Referring back to the house painting example, if Joe knew that you were going to hire the most expensive lawyer in town and knew that those attorney's fees could be thousands of dollars, that certainly would be a significant deterrent for him to file suit. If he lost, he would have to pay more than what his own claim was for. In the American system of justice, a party should not be deterred from bringing a suit for fear that he or she may have to pay the legal fees of the other side if he or she loses.

The philosophy within the American judicial system is that the courts are accessible to any party who feels as though he or she has been wronged by some other person. In earlier times, when one person wronged another there might be a duel in the street to resolve that dispute. Our civilization has evolved to the point where we wish to deter those types of confrontations and encourage parties to resolve their disputes in a civil fashion in front of a judge or jury instead. As such, the *American Rule* does not allow for the recovery of attorney's fees unless stipulated in a written agreement. This is generally considered to be the more democratic rule in that the threat of attorney's fees being awarded should not be a deterrent to a potentially worthy litigant bringing a law suit.

Material Breach

In determining whether one party has failed to comply with the terms of the contract to the point in which damages should be awarded, the court will ask whether the breach of the contract is *material*. A material breach of contract is one that goes to the very heart of the agreement. In the house painting example, the failure to pay the $100 obviously goes to the very heart of the agreement and that failure to pay clearly would be a material breach of contract. If, on the other hand, the painter was one day late in completing the job then, typically, that one day delay would not be a material breach of contract unless the contract contained a *time is of the essence* clause. If such a clause was in the contract, then that means that the parties have expressly agreed that every minute counts. If the party that is required to perform does not perform on time, then

It's the Law

A material breach of contract goes to the very heart of the agreement.

that will be considered a material breach that may bar any right to payment that the parties may have.

Other Contract Theories

As mentioned, the typical contract involves an offer being made, the offer then being accepted by another party, and the exchange of some consideration. There are, however, other theories or means by which a contract may come into existence.

Sometimes a person who is not technically a party to a contract may have rights under the contract if he or she is a *third-party beneficiary*. In order for that beneficiary to enforce the contract with the other parties to the transaction, that beneficiary typically must have been intended by the other parties to benefit from the contract. A typical third-party beneficiary arrangement would be a party who was injured by another person and who then sues that responsible party and makes a claim against their liability insurance policy. The injured person is an intended beneficiary of that responsible party's policy and may sue to enforce payment under the policy.

In some instances, a *quasi-contract* may be recognized. A quasi-contract is a contract implied even though there is no express promise to do anything. In order for a quasi-contract to be recognized, there must have been some benefit conveyed by one party to another. The purpose of recognizing quasi-contracts is to prevent the party receiving the benefit from being *unjustly enriched*.

In addition, the concept known as *promissory estoppel* may be recognized to enforce certain obligations. If certain promises are made and the other person reasonably relies on them and suffers some loss as a result, then under certain circumstances that person may sue to enforce the promise made, even if no actual contract was formed.

Recoverable Damages

The damages that may be provided in a contract action generally fall into two categories—*direct damages* and *indirect damages*. *Direct damages* are those that are actually spelled out in the contract. In the painting example, the $100 that was to be paid would be the direct damages. Suppose Joe told you when he agreed to paint your house that he needed to be paid by a certain date otherwise his landlord was going to evict him from his business location, putting him out of business. If that had been disclosed initially and it was within the contemplation of the parties that Joe would suffer significant consequences if payment was not made in a timely fashion, then those consequential damages—the damages flowing from the failure to pay—may likewise be recoverable in a contract claim as *indirect damages.*

Liquidated Damages

Another form of damage that may be recoverable as part of a breach of a contract claim is what is known as *liquidated damages.* Liquidated damages are expressly set forth in the contract in the event there is a breach. For instance, in many construction contracts it is expressly agreed by the parties that if the contractor does not complete the job by a certain date, he or she will have to pay damages of a fixed amount per day. Liquidated damages are frequently called for in contracts because it may be difficult for the parties to determine what the actual monetary damages are in the event of a breach or, in this case, a delay in performance.

Equitable Relief

Claims for breach of contract, aside from involving claims for money damages, may also involve claims for *equitable relief.* Equitable relief consists of requests by one party to enjoin or dictate either the performance or nonperformance of certain things.

Example: *Suppose Bob enters into a contract with his neighbor to allow a sewer line to be placed across his property so that his neighbor can hook up to the sewer line. However, when the sewer company comes to install the line, Bob decides to stand at the boundary with a shotgun to prevent the excavation. In that instance, Bob may be enjoined from that conduct. The court may order Bob to step aside and allow the excavation to be completed pursuant to the agreement.*

The court in that case would issue an *injunction* requiring Bob to *cease and desist* any behavior that obstructs the excavation. In addition, the neighbor could also sue Bob for money damages since Bob caused the neighbor to have to hire an attorney to file a suit for the injunction. In that circumstance, the attorney's fees might be recoverable.

Checklist for Contracts

In reviewing a written contract, there are several things that you need to be on the lookout for.

- ❏ *The identity of the parties.* Each of the parties needs to be expressly identified. If you are dealing with a corporate entity, you need to make sure the complete name of that corporation is stated in the contract. The only way to confirm that you have the complete name of that corporation is to call the state agency that supervises corporations to get the complete name. In addition, the contract should expressly identify the position of the person signing on behalf of the corporation, so that it is clear that he or she is a corporate officer and therefore has the authority to sign.
- ❏ *Consideration.* The consideration must be expressly stated in the document.
- ❏ *Governing law.* It is a good idea to state in the contract what state's law is going to control this contract in the event there is a dispute that arises. This is important if you are entering into a contract with a person or entity that is not based in the same state where you are.
- ❏ *Time of the essence.* A time of the essence clause is significant if you are interested in prompt performance by the other party. If prompt performance is not a big deal to you, then you may not want a time of the essence clause. If there is a time of the essence clause in the contract and either party does not comply with the time requirements set forth in the contract, then that is considered to be a material breach of the contract.

❑ *Survival.* The term survival means that if one party to the contract were to pass away before there has been complete performance, then the obligation set forth in the contract would apply to the estate and heirs of that person.

❑ *Modification.* It is a good idea to expressly state in the contract that any modification of the contract must be in writing and must be signed by both parties. That eliminates any possibility of there being any oral modification which may be the subject of a later dispute.

❑ *Waiver.* A waiver is an intentional relinquishment of a known right. It is generally a good idea to have a waiver clause in the contract that says that the failure of either party to insist upon strict performance of any of the provisions of this agreement shall not be interpreted as a waiver of any other default or breach of the same or similar nature. This will help prevent a situation in which a waiver of strict performance of a contract provision on one occasion will constitute a waiver of future breaches by that other party.

❑ *Severability.* This term means that if any provision within the agreement is found to be invalid or unenforceable, it will not effect the enforceability or validity of the other provisions in the agreement. Suppose for instance that a particular paragraph in your contract was determined to be either unenforceable or illegal by a court, that conceivably could invalidate your entire contract unless you have this clause within the contract.

❑ *Assignability.* The general rule is that any contract may be assigned unless the contract expressly says otherwise. Assignment of a contract essentially means that you are selling your rights under the contract to another party. For instance, if the contract that you are entering into is a contract for the purchase of an automobile, then you may sign a written contract agreeing to buy that automobile for a certain price. You may then assign it (sell it) to another party unless the contract says that assignment is not allowed. What you are selling in this instance is the contract, not the car. You need to decide whether you want a nonassignment clause within your contract.

❏ *Integration.* An integration clause in a contract says that this contract contains the entire understanding of the parties and that the parties expressly agree that there are no oral or written representations, warranties, or agreements relied upon other than what is expressly said within the written agreement. You may recall the discussion about the parol evidence rule (p.114) that bars the admissibility of any pre-contract discussions that may have taken place between the parties before the contract is actually signed. An integration clause reconfirms that and goes a little bit further to confirm also that any post-contract discussions (discussions or communications that took place after the contract was signed) are not to be relied on by the parties. The word *integration* in this context means that the entire understanding of the parties is integrated into the one document.

❏ *Attorney's Fees.* As previously discussed (see p.116), attorney's fees are typically only recoverable if expressly provided for in the contract or if provided by statute. You should consider whether you want to be able to recover your attorney's fees if a dispute arises and if you do make sure to include an attorney's fee provision within the contract.

Chapter Thirteen

Torts

A *tort* is a civil wrong that is not based upon a contract. If, for example, a person runs a red light and strikes your vehicle (which is lawfully in the intersection), then you could sue that person civilly for the tort of having run the red light. That tort action does not arise out of any contract between you and the other person.

Negligence

There are several different types of torts. The most common tort that you may have some contact with is that of *negligence*. Negligence is a failure to exercise ordinary care.

The concept of negligence is founded upon the idea that a duty is owed from one person to another and there has been a breach of that duty, which then causes an injury or damage to another party. For instance, in the red light example, the duty owed was the duty of not running a red light. If that duty is violated by running the red light and as a result of that you are injured, then all of the elements of a negligence claim have been met.

There are four essential elements to any tort claim.

1. There must be a duty that is owed by the defendant (the party against whom the claim is made) to the plaintiff (the party bringing the claim).
2. There must be a breach or violation of that duty by the defendant.
3. That breach of duty must have then been a proximate cause of injury to the plaintiff.
4. There must be actual injury or damage to the plaintiff.

The first two elements of any tort claim—duty and breach of duty—have just been discussed. The third element of any tort claim is that of proximate cause. *Proximate* is not to be confused with the term *approximate*. Proximate literally means "immediate to, contiguous, touching, or direct." Approximate means not proximate. A proximate cause of an event is one that is *reasonably foreseeable*. If a person runs a red light, then it is reasonably foreseeable that he or she may injure someone. As such, that negligence may be a proximate cause of injury.

> **Example:** *Suppose Alan is playing a game of catch with his son in front of his house. His wind-up is a bit too aggressive and he overthrows the ball. The ball goes through the front window of your home and then through the rear window of your home striking a barbecue stove that is on your back porch. The stove then falls off the back porch, rolls down the hill, and kills another neighbor. What is Alan responsible for?*

The first question is whether Alan was negligent. Alan probably was negligent for throwing the ball so hard that it broke the front window of your home. The next question is whether that negligence was a proximate cause of injury to your home. Clearly it was.

The final question is whether or not that negligence was a proximate cause of injury to your neighbor. That is a tougher question. It comes down to essentially an issue of whether it was reasonably foreseeable that by throwing the ball as hard as he did, it would not only go through your front window, but also the back window, and then strike your barbecue oven, knock it off the back porch, and cause it to roll down the hill and strike your neighbor. That type of resulting injury is probably not reasonably foreseeable, and as such the *chain of causation* would have been broken at some point in that sequence of events. Typically, in that type of case, the question of proximate cause would be submitted to a jury for resolution as to whether Alan's negligence was a proximate cause of injury to your neighbor.

The fourth and final element of any tort claim is that of damages or injuries incurred. To justify a recovery of any substantial amount, the injuries or damages must be more than minimal. Those injuries may include medical expenses, lost wages, pain and suffering, humiliation, etc.

Motor Vehicle Accident

The most common form of tort claim arises from automobile collisions. Those tort claims normally involve some careless or reckless act by one driver resulting in a collision with another motor vehicle. Whether the operation of a motor vehicle involves actual negligence depends upon how the driver's conduct is viewed in the light of the *Rules of the Road* as set forth either in your state code or local code governing traffic regulations. The rules of the road or traffic regulations establish the standards for operation of motor vehicles. A violation of these rules or regulations typically constitutes negligence.

Motor vehicle accidents involving common carriers (buses, taxis, trains, and planes) may have a set of rules that are slightly different than what would apply to an automobile. Common carriers are frequently held to a very high degree of care. As such, if there is even slight negligence on their part that contributes to the injury of one of their passengers, then the common carrier may be liable.

Premises Liability

Another area of the law that produces many tort claims is *premises liability*. A person who is lawfully on someone else's premises and who is injured as a result of some negligence of that property owner may have a claim against the property owner. The duty or standard of care to which the property owner is held may depend on the status of the injured person.

The different statuses that may apply are that of *invitee*, *licensee*, or *trespasser*. An *invitee* is typically someone who comes onto the property for some legitimate business purpose. A *licensee* may generally be thought of as a social guest. A *trespasser* is someone who is not allowed on the premises and who is there without the knowledge or consent of the property owner.

Exactly what duty is owed by the property owner to each of these different classes of persons may vary dramatically from state to state. The general rule of law, however, is that a property owner has a duty to exercise ordinary care to keep his or her premises in a reasonably safe condition. When an owner fails to exercise that ordinary care and someone who is lawfully on the premises is injured as a result, the property owner may be liable.

One thing that distinguishes premises liability claims from other types of tort claims is that the party who is injured (the plaintiff) must prove that the property owner had *notice* of the defective condition on the premises. For instance, if your daughter slips and falls on a banana peel that was on the floor in the school cafeteria, she does not necessarily have a basis for a claim against the school system or the company that runs the cafeteria. She must present some evidence of how long that banana peel had been on the floor in order to prevail on such a claim. If it turns out that the banana peel had only been there a short period of time and was there because of the actions of some other student in the school, the school may not have had a reasonable opportunity to see the banana peel and clean it up. Thus, there may not be any negligence on the part of that school.

It's the Law

A property owner can only exercise ordinary care toward defects or deficiencies that he or she has knowledge of.

The logic of this rule is that a property owner is not necessarily a guarantor of the safety of all persons on his or her premises but is simply required to exercise ordinary care. A property owner can only exercise *ordinary care* as to those defects or deficiencies that he or she has some knowledge of or that he or she should have known of.

In the case of your daughter, she must prove that the banana peel had been on the floor long enough that the school system or the manager of the cafeteria should have known that the banana peel was on the floor. The school system or cafeteria manager should therefore have cleaned it up or placed signs out to warn customers of the presence of the object on the floor.

If the banana peel was placed on the floor either intentionally or accidently by an *employee* of the entity that operates the school cafeteria or by an employee of the school system, then your daughter may not have to prove that entity had notice of the presence of the banana peel on the floor. The negligence of the employee in placing it there would simply be *imputed* to the employer.

Take another example of a premises liability claim.

Example: *Suppose you are the tenant in a large apartment building where there have been a series of crimes committed resulting in serious personal injuries to the occupants. The property owner is aware of those crimes, but takes no steps to warn other tenants of the crime wave in that building and likewise takes no steps to improve security in the building. If you are subsequently assaulted and injured as a result of a person coming onto the premises for the purpose of committing a crime, then you may have a claim against that landlord based upon a negligence theory. That is, the landlord knew or should have known that there was a danger to the tenants, yet the landlord took no steps to either warn the tenants or to decrease the security risk to the tenants.*

Look at that claim from the point of view of how the four elements of a tort claim apply. The first element of a tort claim is the establishment of a duty owed by the defendant to the plaintiff. The duty in this case arises out of the relationship of the parties. That is, the property owner or the landlord owes a duty of reasonable care to persons who are lawfully on the premises.

It's the Law
Reasonable care is that degree of care that a prudent person would exercise in a given circumstance.

You may ask, *what is reasonable care?* Reasonable care is whatever a jury says it is. A textbook definition of reasonable care is that degree of care that a prudent person would exercise in that circumstance. If the landlord in this instance failed to take some steps to warn the tenants or persons lawfully on the premises of the criminal incidents occurring, then that may be evidence of a breach of the duty to exercise reasonable care and fulfill the second element. If the assault in question was perpetrated by some person who was unlawfully on the premises, then the third element of a tort claim has been met in that the breach of duty has been shown to be a cause of injury. The final element of a tort claim is simply that of injury or damage. In this case, the injury or damage consists of the personal injury to the plaintiff.

Product Liability

A *product liability* claim is one in which a person contends that a particular product is defective in some way and that defect has caused injury. You may recall a famous product liability claim that was brought against Ford Motor Company many years ago relating to its Pinto automobiles. Ford made an engineering decision to place the gas tank on the Pinto in the rear of the vehicle, even though it knew that placing the gas tank in this location could result in serious injury to the occupants if the vehicle was involved in a rear-end collision.

Documentation was produced during litigation that Ford knew or should have known of that risk, yet made a conscious decision to continue to keep those vehicles on the road because it felt the overall financial benefit would weigh in its favor, even if it had to pay several million dollars in claims as a result of injuries.

The jury in one of those cases returned a very substantial award against Ford Motor Company for compensatory damages for the injuries suffered by the plaintiff. The jury also awarded substantial punitive damages to punish Ford for its wrongful conduct in not taking the vehicles off the road or warning the public of the dangers associated with that vehicle.

Another fairly well known product liability case involved a McDonald's restaurant. In that case, an elderly woman purchased a cup of coffee from a drive-in window at McDonald's. She apparently placed that cup of coffee between her legs and subsequently spilled the coffee. The case received a good deal of attention because it was touted by the insurance industry as an example of a runaway jury verdict. In fact, the insurance industry failed to disclose to the public that in that particular case the *plaintiff* had made an attempt to settle the case simply for her medical bills, which were substantial because she was hospitalized for over a week. McDonald's, however, refused to entertain any reasonable settlement offers.

The evidence that was presented at trial was that McDonald's had been warned on many occasions that their coffee was approximately twenty degrees hotter than what was recommended by the local health department and was so hot that it could cause third degree burns. In fact, the coffee served by McDonald's was not just hot (135° to 140°), but at 180° to 190° was able to cook through all layers of skin within seven seconds. McDonald's admitted that its coffee was 40° to 50° hotter than is fit for human consumption and knew that more than seven hundred people, including babies, had been burned by its coffee. McDonald's, however, refused to reduce the temperature of its coffee because it felt it sold more coffee at that level than it would at a lesser temperature.

The plaintiff in this case was an elderly woman who suffered third degree burns over 6% of her body. The state where that case was tried was a *comparative negligence* state (see p.139). As such, the jury, having found the plaintiff partially negligent because of how she carried the coffee, reduced her verdict by a proportion that was due to her own negligence.

In addition to awarding a compensatory damage amount, the jury also awarded punitive damages against McDonald's equal to its gross receipts of two days of coffee sales in order to teach it a lesson. The actual verdict in that case was $200,000 for compensatory damages and $2.7 million in punitive damages. The punitive damage award was reduced by the court on a post-trial motion to $480,000. As a result of that verdict, McDonald's reduced the temperature of its coffee.

A product liability claim may be founded upon negligence principles, but it may also raise a legal theory known as *breach of warranty*. Within the sale of a product there is either an express or implied warranty that the product is reasonably fit for the purpose for which it is sold. If it turns out that the product is not reasonably fit for that purpose, then that may constitute a breach of warranty and may give rise to a claim for damages if someone is injured as a result of that breach of warranty. Breach of warranty claims technically are contract claims, but they may be asserted as part of a product liability lawsuit.

Normally, in a product liability claim, the plaintiff will need to present some expert testimony as to what the defect is in the product. For instance, in the Ford Pinto case, the plaintiff had to present expert testimony from engineers to establish that the placement of the gas tank in the rear of the vehicle was dangerous and was not good engineering.

Professional Liability

Professional liability claims may come in the form of medical malpractice actions, legal malpractice actions, accounting malpractice claims, or architectural malpractice actions. In many states, the medical profession has been granted certain special protections. For instance, some states have imposed a cap or a limitation on the amount of money that can be recovered against any doctor or health care provider as a result of their negligence. The reason for that cap on damages is to help hold down the cost of medical malpractice insurance coverage for health care providers.

In addition, some states have imposed special requirements that must be met before a doctor or a health care provider can be sued. In some cases the plaintiff must have the claim reviewed by a medical malpractice review panel that makes a preliminary determination whether the claim has any merit. The decision rendered by the medical malpractice review panel may in some instances be admissible in evidence if the case is tried in front of a jury.

A professional liability claim is different from any other type of tort claim that may be asserted. With these types of claims, the plaintiff typically has to present testimony from a witness who has some expertise in that field as to the *standard of care* that should have been adhered to by that professional person. Evidence must then be presented as to the breach of that standard of care and how that breach caused damage to the plaintiff.

In a medical malpractice action, that testimony typically comes from another medical doctor in the same field of expertise as the defendant that is being sued. The same concept applies normally in legal malpractice actions and also in architectural malpractice actions. There could be some instances when expert testimony would not be necessary because the negligence is so obvious that there is no need to bring an expert witness into court to explain the technical aspects of the case.

For instance, if a patient goes into the hospital for an operation on the right knee and the doctor ends up operating on the left knee, there is no need for expert testimony to establish that the standard of care is that the doctor should have operated on the right knee. Any reasonable person would know that the operation on the left knee was unnecessary and therefore was negligent on the doctor's part.

Standard of Care

In most negligence claims, the issue of standard of care arises. In an automobile accident case, the standard of care is defined by the traffic regulations. For instance, the traffic regulations dictate that you shall not enter an intersection on a red light. That regulation establishes the standard of care by which all persons are bound in terms of passing through an intersection. In other contexts there may be building codes or other state or local codes that establish the standard of care by which property owners are bound. Those codes can be the basis upon which a negligence case may be founded because they establish the standard of care to which the defendant is held. If the defendant has violated that code, then that may be evidence of a breach of duty by that defendant. If that breach resulted in damage to you, then you may have a basis for a negligence claim against the property owner.

The concept of standard of care becomes especially important in certain types of professional liability claims—medical malpractice claims, legal malpractice claims, or architectural malpractice claims. In those types of claims, the plaintiff has to establish what the standard of care is. The standard of care is established by means of the presentation of evidence by experts in that field. For instance, if in the course of your heart surgery the surgeon happens to penetrate your coronary artery with a catheter and you suffer irreparable damage, has the standard of care for that procedure been violated? That is not something a nonmedical person could answer. Therefore, it is not something that a group of jurors could answer as nonmedical people unless they hear evidence from a medical expert establishing what the standard of care is.

The standard of care in that particular instance may be that the surgeon, through the use of radiological instruments, should have been able to tell where the catheter was going and therefore should have known when he or she was about to puncture the arterial wall. The surgeon could have avoided the rupture if he or she had been attentive to the radiological instrument that showed where the catheter was.

In that instance, the standard of care evidence presented by the plaintiff may show that the doctor was negligent in puncturing the arterial wall with that catheter. You can rest assured that the defendant doctor will bring in his own medical expert who will refute that and who will state that there is no breach of the standard of care in this circumstance. It was simply an unfortunate accident that happened and there was no negligence on the part of the doctor.

Proximate Cause

In addition to proving that there was a breach of the standard of care by a doctor, the plaintiff must also show that the breach was a proximate cause of the plaintiff's injury. In the example of the puncture of the arterial wall by the catheter, the defendant may argue that even if that was negligence, the patient only had a 5% chance of survival and therefore was probably going to die anyhow. As such, any negligence that may have been committed was really irrelevant. This is a frequent defense raised in professional negligence claims and is frequently one that has some merit—the doctor may have been negligent, but the patient would have died anyhow. This reemphasizes the importance of the concept of proximate cause. That is, even though the doctor may have been negligent, the negligence may not have been a cause of injury since the patient may have suffered dire consequences in any event.

Children

Many tort claims that are brought involve children. Children, in general, are given a *favored status* in the law, meaning that they have special protection. This is likewise true in regard to tort claims. For instance, in regard to negligence claims, children under 7 years of age are generally legally incapable of committing any act of negligence.

Children between the ages of 7 and 14 are generally presumed to be incapable of committing negligence, although that presumption can be rebutted with the presentation of evidence showing that the child is capable of committing a negligent act because of his or her intelligence level, experience level, or other factors that may bear on that.

Attractive Nuisance

You have probably heard of the term *attractive nuisance*. That is a concept of negligence that is recognized in many states. An attractive nuisance is an object that by its very location and configuration is attractive and also dangerous to children. If the owner of that object allows it to remain accessible to children, knowing that it will attract them and knowing that they probably will be injured if they come in contact with it, that may be a basis for a negligence claim against the owner of that object.

Res Ipsa Loquitur

Literally, the term *res ipsa loquitur* means *the thing speaks for itself.*
Res ipsa loquitur is a rule of evidence that states that a jury may
conclude that a defendant is negligent if:

- the plaintiff has been injured as a result of an instrumentality (some tool or object) that is in the exclusive control of
  that defendant;
- the defendant has or should have exclusive knowledge of
  the way that instrumentality was used; and,
- the injury is one that would not normally have occurred if
  the instrument had been used properly.

Example: *Suppose you are walking down the street and a dresser
drawer falls on your head. It so happens that the dresser
drawer came from the apartment window above. It had
been placed there by the tenant who was doing some spring
cleaning and the tenant accidentally bumped the dresser
drawer. Have the elements of* **res ipsa loquitur** *been met
in that instance?*

*They probably have been, in that the dresser drawer was in
the exclusive control of the defendant, the defendant had
exclusive knowledge as to how the dresser drawer was used,
and finally the injury is one that would not normally have
occurred if the dresser drawer had been used properly. As
long as you can prove those basic elements, you probably
would be entitled to recover money against that tenant for
his or her negligence.*

Vicarious Liability

A significant concept within tort law is *vicarious liability.* The concept of vicarious liability means a principal may be liable for the
conduct or the misconduct of his or her agents. That principal/
agent relationship arises in the employment context between an
employer and an employee. It may also arise in other contexts

involving contractors. From a plaintiff's point of view, the concept of vicarious liability is important because it typically is that legal concept that allows for complete recovery of damages. For instance, if you are rear-ended by a truck driven by an employee of the ABC Company, your attorney would file the claim against not only the driver, but also the employer. If suit was filed only against the driver and it turns out that there was no insurance covering that vehicle, then whatever judgment you got against the driver might be uncollectible simply because the driver might not have the financial resources to pay the judgment. If, however, you get the judgment also against the employer, then that employer probably would have the financial resources either in the form of insurance coverage or otherwise to satisfy the judgment.

The employer in that case is liable for the conduct of the employee, assuming that the employee was acting within the scope of his or her employment. If, on the other hand, the employee was on a personal mission while operating a company vehicle and the employer had no knowledge of it and had not consented to it, then there may be no vicarious liability. Perhaps the employee was acting on his or her own and was not doing anything on behalf of the employer at the time of the collision.

The concept of vicarious liability has been the subject of a good deal of litigation over the years.

Example: Suppose an insurance salesman comes into your home to sell you insurance on behalf of the XYZ Company. He presents to you his business card along with all the brochures of the XYZ Company. He convinces you that based upon the extensive advertising of that Company and because of the well recognized name that this is a very reputable company. Based on that you purchase a policy of insurance and tender a check in a substantial amount. If the salesman then absconds with the money, is the XYZ Company liable for your loss?

They probably are even though that salesman may not be a direct employee of the company. The salesman in that instance may be an independent contractor, but the XYZ Company is probably still liable because it is the one who gave that salesman all the trappings of authenticity, gave him the opportunity to engage in his fraudulent behavior, and essentially set the whole process in motion through the use of its company name and company advertising.

Strict Liability

Strict liability means that the defendant is liable for his or her conduct in certain instances, even without a showing of actual negligence, if that conduct was a cause of injury to the plaintiff. Strict liability normally only arises in regard to activities that are extremely dangerous. For instance, if you are operating a quarry and in the course of blasting with dynamite you damage the home of one of your neighbors, that neighbor may not have to prove that there was any negligence on your part in the blasting operation, but simply has to prove that the blasting was the cause of damage to his or her home. In that circumstance, the party conducting the blasting may be strictly liable for any damage that results from that dangerous activity.

Intentional Torts

Aside from the types of claims mentioned previously, there are several *intentional torts* that can be asserted. Those intentional torts consist of such claims as assault and battery, conversion, defamation, false imprisonment, fraud, malicious prosecution, invasion of privacy, trespass, and the intentional infliction of emotional distress. All these claims have specific elements that must be met and proved for a plaintiff to prevail.

A *battery* is simply an unwanted touching of one person by another. *Conversion* is the taking of a person's property without that person's consent. (Conversion in the civil system is similar to *larceny* in the criminal system.)

Defamation can come in either written (*libel*) or oral (*slander*) form and consists of making injurious statements about a person that are untrue. If the injurious statements involve an imputation of a criminal offense, involve moral turpitude, impute a contagious disease, impute unfitness to perform the duties of office, or include words that prejudice a person in his or her profession or trade, then they may be referred to as being *defamatory per se*.

If the alleged statement is not defamatory *per se*, then the plaintiff may have to prove what are called *special damages* in order to recover against the defendant. Special damages would come in the form of out-of-pocket expenses incurred as a result of those defamatory statements.

Example: *If you are a surgeon and David calls you a butcher, that is a statement that is defamatory* per se. *You could assert a defamation claim against David even though you may not have incurred any special damages (any out-of-pocket expense as a result of the making of that statement).*

Keep in mind that truth is always a complete defense to a defamation claim.

If, on the other hand, you are unemployed and Sarah calls you a crook, and as a result of making that comment you incur so much emotional distress that you seek psychiatric help, you may have a basis for a defamation claim against Sarah. Even though the comment made

It's the Law
The truth is always a complete defense to a defamation claim.

is not defamatory *per se*, the fact that you have incurred medical expenses as a result of Sarah making the comment about you satisfies the special damages requirement. It gives you the basis for a defamation claim against Sarah.

Some statements, although defamatory, are protected by a *qualified* or *absolute privilege*. For instance, a statement made by an employer about an employee to a new prospective employer may be governed by a *qualified privilege*. The idea is to allow employers to freely exchange information about employees. What that means is that the employee in a defamation action against the former employer may have to claim and prove that there actually was some malice in the statements that were made.

An *absolute privilege* would be one that is an absolute bar to a claim for defamation. For instance, comments made in the course of a judicial proceeding are generally governed by such a privilege. The idea is to allow the parties to freely exchange comments during such a proceeding.

Claims of *false imprisonment* and *malicious prosecution* arise in the context of a person improperly restraining another person or initiating a criminal prosecution that is subsequently found to be unjustified.

Fraud is the intentional misrepresentation of a material fact made for the purpose of inducing reliance and that does induce reliance to the detriment or damage of the plaintiff. Fraud is a very difficult thing to prove. Unlike most civil claims that must be proven simply by a *preponderance of the evidence* or what is referred to as the *greater weight of the evidence*, fraud claims must be proved by clear and convincing evidence, which is a much higher standard and much more difficult to prove. The reason for the higher standard of proof in fraud claims is that the law recognizes fraud as an offense involving surreptitious behavior that may be subject to different interpretations. It is therefore felt that the plaintiff should have a more difficult burden of proof in these types of claims than would apply in the run-of-the-mill tort claims that may be asserted.

Another intentional tort is called the *intentional infliction of emotional distress*. To pursue such a claim, you must prove that the conduct of the defendant was intentional and outrageous, that the conduct caused emotional distress, and that the emotional distress was severe. It is often difficult to meet all of these elements.

There are also a number of intentional "business torts." For example, interference with economic relations requires the plaintiff to prove that he or she had a business relationship (or business expectancy) that the defendant was aware of and the defendant acted intentionally and improperly to discontinue that relationship or prevent that expectancy from being realized.

Damages

The final element of any tort claim that must be established is *damages*. Damages may be thought of as the injury incurred. The injury may come in the form of personal injury such as a broken arm or leg, pain and suffering, emotional distress, medical expenses, lost wages, or permanent disability. *Pain and suffering* is an elusive concept. The words themselves best define the concept. When you are physically injured, it would be expected that you would experience some pain, anguish, or emotional stress. Normally, a jury in an injury case is called upon to award a monetary amount for that pain and suffering along with the other damages that are claimed.

Joint and Several Liability

Another important principle in liability in a tort action is *joint and several liability*. Under the principle of joint and several liability, each defendant is 100% liable for the judgment that is rendered. This principle has been under a good deal of attack lately because it can create circumstances wherein a defendant can wind up paying more than his or her fair share of any judgment, especially if the other defendant cannot afford to pay.

Joint and several liability is something that is well ingrained into our legal system. The rationale behind it is to make sure that the plaintiff can obtain full recovery for whatever judgment is entered. It then becomes the burden of the defendants against whom the judgment has been entered to fight among themselves as to any eventual sharing of that liability.

Comparative and Contributory Negligence

Different states have different ways of dealing with negligence claims. Some of them acknowledge the concept of *comparative negligence*, while other states are known as *contributory negligence* jurisdictions. In a *comparative negligence jurisdiction*, the negligence may be compared between the parties. For instance, going back to the red light example, if you happened to be intoxicated and laying in the middle of the intersection when you were struck, then there obviously would be some negligence on your part. The jury would be called upon to compare the different levels of negligence.

In that example, the jury might conclude that the driver was 50% negligent and you were also 50% negligent. If the jury then determined that your total damages were $100,000, you would only receive $50,000, because you were 50% negligent.

In a *contributory negligence jurisdiction* there is no comparison of negligence. This means that if you were negligent by 1%, and that negligence was a cause of your damage, then your claim is barred and you receive nothing. Contributory negligence is a principle derived from the common law that is still recognized in some states. It is indeed a very harsh principle of law and in many instances is unfair to people who are probably entitled to recover something for their damages, but may not be entitled to 100% compensation.

Defenses

There are several *affirmative defenses* that may be raised in regard to a tort claim. An *affirmative defense* is a defense that may be raised by a defendant that constitutes a complete bar to a claim. One of those affirmative defenses is that of the *statute of limitations*. Every state has set forth a statute of limitations for virtually every type of civil claim, whether it be a tort claim, contract claim, or otherwise. If the claim is not asserted within the time allowed by that statute, then the claim is deemed to be barred. The assertion of a claim is accomplished in most states by actually filing a lawsuit at the courthouse. Some states require actual service of the suit papers upon the defendant before the statute of limitations runs.

Another defense that may be asserted in a tort case is that of *assumption of the risk*. Assumption of the risk arises when the plaintiff understands the nature of the risk involved and voluntarily assumes that risk.

Example: *If you decide to go out to the supermarket during the middle of a very bad ice storm, recognizing that the roads and walkways are not navigable, and while walking from your car to the store, you slip and fall, then you probably have assumed the risk of an injury. You knew that there was a risk associated with going out during those weather conditions and you voluntarily chose to accept that risk.*

Immunities

Several states still recognize various types of *immunities*. That immunity may come in the form of sovereign immunity, charitable immunity, or family immunity. *Sovereign immunity* is based upon the concept that the king cannot be sued. In the United States that means the sovereign or the government cannot be sued. Many jurisdictions have waived that immunity either in whole or in part. If the local or state governmental entity that you are planning on suing is deemed by state law to be immune from tort claims, then you may not be able to sue that entity at all unless it expressly chooses to waive its immunity. Many governmental entities by means of state law have expressly waived their immunity either entirely or have allowed claims to be asserted against them up to certain dollar amounts. (This varies from state to state.)

Charitable immunity is a doctrine that applies in many states to organizations that are truly charitable. A charitable organization is generally considered to be one that fulfills a strictly charitable function and does not make any attempt to collect its debts. Charitable organizations may be immune from tort claims. For instance, if you were injured on the premises of the Red Cross because of some negligence on their part, depending on the law in that particular state, the Red Cross may have the defense of charitable immunity to your claim because they truly are a charitable organization.

There are certain states that still recognize elements of *family immunity*. That is, tort claims may not be asserted against parents or siblings for certain types of behavior.

Wrongful Death Actions

If the injury suffered results in the death of a person, then that person's estate may assert a *wrongful death claim*. A wrongful death claim occurs when the injured party, rather than having simply suffered personal injury, has actually died as a result of the misconduct of the defendant. A wrongful death claim may be based upon a negligence theory, a breach of warranty theory or an intentional tort theory such as assault and battery.

Wrongful death claims are a fairly recent phenomenon. Common law did not recognize wrongful death claims on the theory that once a person had died, there was no amount of money that could compensate for the loss. As such, a person's claim died with him or her. However, over the years, the state legislatures have come to recognize that even though death may bring an end to the suffering and damages incurred by the decedent, there may be persons left behind who have been damaged and may continue to be damaged in the future as a result of the passing of the decedent.

Every state has its own wrongful death statute that defines exactly what damages are recoverable under the wrongful death act. Typically the damages recoverable are damages consisting of solace and grief experienced by the survivors, loss of earnings suffered by the dependents from the decedent's subsequent inability to generate income, any medical expenses incurred by the decedent, and funeral expenses.

Chapter Fourteen

Domestic Relations

The field of *domestic relations* law is sometimes loosely referred to as divorce law or family law. Domestic relations, however, covers much more than simply entry of a divorce decree. It covers such things as the award of custody of minor children, the payment of spousal and child support, and the distribution of property in the event of a divorce.

Marriage

There are two types of marriage that may be recognized—a *common law marriage* and a *ceremonial marriage*. (The law differs from state-to-state as to whether common law marriage is recognized.) A *common law marriage* is a marriage in which a couple has lived together for the required period of time (typically seven years) and has publicly held themselves out to be husband and wife. They may do that by not only sharing the same household and the same bed, but perhaps by even sharing the same last name, having children, referring to each other as husband and wife, and engaging in all of the typical activities that one might attribute to a married couple. If those requirements are met, then that couple is deemed in the eyes of the law of that state to be married.

A *ceremonial marriage* is conducted by an authorized minister, justice of the peace, or other designated official who has the authority granted by the state to conduct civil marriage ceremonies.

Annulment

A means by which a marriage may be terminated is through *annulment*. The grounds for annulment are defined by state law.

It's the Law
The law considers an annulled marriage to have never existed at all.

Those grounds may be things such as lack of capacity due to being underage, fraudulent misrepresentation of intent in entering into the marriage as evidenced by a failure to ever consummate the marriage, insanity, or failure to disclose a prior felony conviction. Annulment is different from divorce in that instead of ending the marriage, the law considers the marriage to have never existed at all.

Divorce

Once a couple is deemed to be married, whether it be by common law or means of ceremony, that marriage may be terminated only by a decree of a court. The *divorce decree* does not necessarily have to be entered in the state where the parties were married. Quite frequently one or both parties may change their residence in order to come within the jurisdiction of another state or foreign country to have a *quickie divorce* entered. Those types of divorce decrees may be valid provided there was a *bona fide* change in residence and provided proper notice was given to the other spouse of the fact that the marriage was to be terminated.

Grounds

A divorce may be decreed either on *fault grounds* or *no-fault grounds*. The *fault grounds* for a divorce are adultery, constructive desertion, cruelty, and actual desertion. A *no-fault divorce* means that there is no attribution of fault to the other party, but simply that the parties have lived separate and apart for the period of time required by state law with the intent to terminate the marriage.

Adultery is the act of engaging in sexual relations with a person other than your spouse during the marriage. Adultery is difficult to prove. It is rare that the offending spouse is actually caught *in the act*. More often the jilted spouse has the offending spouse followed by private detectives who then photograph or otherwise record the conduct of the offending spouse going to the home of the paramour, spending the night there, and then exiting the following morning. The court will generally accept that as evidence of the fact that an illicit affair is going on.

Desertion is the intentional departure from the family home without the consent of the other spouse. *Constructive desertion* may exist where one spouse has created circumstances within the family home so intolerable as to be deemed to have deserted the marriage, even though he or she still physically resides in the home. That conduct may come in the form of abuse, denial of sexual relations, or other egregious conduct that essentially results in a termination of the marriage. A final fault grounds for divorce is *cruelty*, which comes in the form of mental abuse or physical abuse.

Corroboration Requirement

One thing that distinguishes divorce proceedings from most other types of civil claims is that there generally is a requirement of *corroboration* of the basic elements of the divorce claim. That is, the parties alone cannot prove the grounds for divorce. Many states require that the testimony of one or both parties be corroborated by a third person in order to establish the grounds for divorce. For instance, in an adultery action, one spouse simply saying that she saw the other spouse engaged in sexual relations with a third person is not sufficient to establish adultery. Instead that evidence must be corroborated by a third person. The third person could be the paramour or, more often, a private detective.

The rationale behind this requirement of corroboration is that the state has an interest in preserving marriage and therefore the parties themselves should not be allowed through their own testimony or evidence to terminate the marriage. There has been a movement over the years to liberalize the basis for divorce throughout the United States. Some states are actually trying to make it more difficult for parties to divorce by providing a longer waiting period before a divorce may be decreed.

Many states still classify divorce actions as *a mensa et thoro* or divorce *a vinculo matrimonii*. A divorce *a mensa et thoro* is literally a divorce from bed and board, which is a type of legal separation that may continue until the final decree of divorce is entered. The final decree comes in the form of a divorce *a vinculo matrimonii* (from the bonds of matrimony). That final decree of divorce is entered after the statutory separation period has been satisfied or, in some cases, based upon some fault grounds such as adultery. A divorce *a mensa et thoro* enables the parties to get a legal separation when they are unable to get a full divorce due to religious reasons or other circumstances.

Defenses

The party against whom a divorce action is brought may raise certain defenses to that claim. Those defenses may consist of such things as:

- condonation;
- consent;
- justification;
- laches;
- reconciliation; and,
- recrimination.

Condonation is the act of forgiving the marital offense. For instance, if a husband learns that his wife has engaged in adultery and thereafter takes her back to the marital bed, that is deemed to be a condonation of the marital offense of adultery. Likewise, if one party *consents* to the other party leaving the marital home, that is a defense to a desertion claim. If one party has engaged in egregious conduct that justifies the departure of the other spouse from the marital home, that may constitute *justification*.

Laches is a type of statute of limitations defense, but it is not governed by an express code section that sets forth a precise period of time within which a claim may be brought. You may recall the earlier discussion about law claims and equitable claims (see pp. 35–36). Divorce actions are deemed to be equitable claims because typically the parties do not sue for an express monetary amount, but rather they ask the court to award certain forms of equitable relief—the awarding of a divorce, the awarding of custody, or the distribution of marital property.

Example: *Mike sues Mary on fault grounds. He does so after a sub-stantial period of time has elapsed after the fault conduct occurred. As a result of that lapse of time, Mary is preju-diced due to the loss of witnesses or loss of evidence. This situation may give rise to the defense of laches.*

Other defenses that may be raised are *reconciliation* and *recrim-ination*. Reconciliation is essentially the fact that the parties have gotten back together. Recrimination as a defense may be appli-cable where the spouse bringing the claim has likewise engaged in conduct that may be the basis for divorce and that constitutes a defense to the claim.

Custody

Although the goal of most domestic relations work is to obtain a final decree of divorce, there are many additional facets to domestic relations work. If there are any children of the mar-riage, the court will have to award *custody* to one or both parties as part of that final decree of divorce. Typically the court will also fix monetary amounts for *child support* awards and *spousal sup-port* awards if necessary.

Years ago, many courts recognized a presumption in custody issues that favored the mother. She was presumed to be the appropriate parent to whom custody should be awarded. The father would then be awarded *visitation rights*. He could have the children in his physical control at the times allowed by terms of the court decree. Other than those visitation rights, the father frequently had no other rights. For instance, a father typi-cally would not have the right to talk to the children's teacher to inquire how they were doing, be involved in their sports activities, or even have access to their medical records.

In the last several years, custody arrangements have been liberalized, so today a more common arrangement is an award of *joint legal custody*. This means that each parent retains full parental rights to be involved in the lives of their children, although one parent will be granted primary, *physical custody* of the children. The other parent then will have custody (or what otherwise might have been referred to as visitation) during designated times that are established by the court or agreed to by the parties.

The general rule of thumb that the court applies in awarding custody is to determine what is truly in the *best interest of the child.*

When custody is contested between the parties, the court will look at a number of different factors in deciding which parent should have primary, physical custody. Those factors may include such things as:

♦ the employment status of the parents;
♦ capability of providing for day care;
♦ the amount of spare time that the parent will have to be involved in the lives of the children;
♦ who has possession of the family home;
♦ how the children are doing in their school and neighborhood;
♦ the financial status of the parties;
♦ any mental or emotional difficulties manifested by either party; and,
♦ to some extent the wishes of the child (depending upon the age of the child). The older the child is, the more likely it is that the court will entertain evidence regarding the wishes of the child.

It's the Law
Grandparents may also have visitation rights.

Grandparents may also have visitation rights. The right of grandparent visitation normally will not be to the detriment of either parent, but instead will typically be allowed during the period of time when the related parent has actual physical control of the child.

A law known as the *Uniform Child Custody Jurisdiction and Enforcement Act* has been adopted throughout the United States in order to provide some uniformity among the various state courts in awarding custody of children. That uniform act creates disincentives to parents to abduct or secretly remove children from one jurisdiction to another for the purpose of obtaining a more favorable forum in which to litigate their dispute. In addition, it assures that the custody determinations made by one state court will be recognized in other state courts.

A concept that is often overlooked in custody determinations is *domestic violence*. A good bit has been written about this issue and most states now recognize the existence of domestic violence as an important factor in the determination of which parent should have custody. The parent who perpetrates the domestic violence, in many instances, may not be the appropriate person to have custody. Due to the destructive impact he or she has had on the family unit, the propensity for children who witness spousal abuse to perpetuate that behavior is increased.

Change of Custody

It is not unusual after a final decree of divorce has been entered that the noncustodial parent files a motion with the court requesting a change of custody to award him or her primary, physical custody of the child. Such a motion is generally based upon there having been some material change in circumstance affecting the interests of the child.

Once custody has been awarded to one party, it generally takes some fairly egregious conduct on the part of the custodial parent or some significant change in circumstance to justify a change in custody. The prevailing wisdom is that even though the current arrangement may not be perfect, children tend to crave stability in their lives. Therefore, the court must hear some compelling evidence before it will change that otherwise stable arrangement.

Adoption and Paternity

Other issues that a domestic relations court may be called upon to decide relate to *adoption* and *legitimacy of children*. *Adoption* procedures are strictly governed by state law. The court supervises that adoption procedure to ensure that the new adoptive parents are fit and appropriate persons to have custody of the child. The procedure involves an initial review of the adoptive parents before they actually receive the child. Then there is a period of time when the child will be allowed to be with the new parents on an interim basis. Then the entire situation will be reviewed again before a final order of adoption is entered. Once a final order of adoption is entered, the adoptive child acquires the same status as a natural child of that couple.

Another issue that may arise in the course of domestic relations litigation is that of *legitimacy* or *paternity*. If a man has fathered a child, then the mother has a right to claim child support from the father. If the couple is not married, then there may be an issue as to parentage. That is fairly easily resolved through blood testing. Once parentage is established, then the father or noncustodial parent will be ordered to provide child support based upon his or her income level and the needs of the child.

Child Support

In awarding child support, either in a divorce action or in a paternity action, the court looks at several factors to determine what the amount of that support will be—the respective income of the parties, the financial needs of the parties, and whether the parties are fully employed or are underemployed. Many states now have statutory guidelines for child support amounts. Those guidelines are published in the state code and they are based upon the gross income of the parties. A formula is then applied in order to determine exactly what amount of child support is due from the parent who does not have primary custody.

Spousal Support

Either party to a divorce action may also make a request for *spousal support* or what has traditionally been known as *alimony*. This is something that may be claimed by either the husband or the wife. The general rule of thumb is that the principal breadwinner in the family is obliged to maintain the other party in the style of life to which they have become accustomed during the course of the marriage. As a practical matter, that often is not possible. If a couple was living on $45,000 a year before the divorce and the husband is the sole breadwinner in the family, then once they divorce there obviously will be a reduction in lifestyle.

Property Division

The *distribution of property* acquired during the course of the marriage is another issue that a domestic relations court is called upon to resolve as part of a divorce action. The distribution of property can become very complicated when you are dealing with pieces of real estate, stocks and bonds that have appreciated in value, or pensions and retirement plans. These frequently require an analysis by a CPA or an economist to determine their total value. Recommendations then must be made to the court as to how each party has contributed to the increase in value of those assets and what the total value of the assets are.

For instance, if the parties have been married for twenty years and if during the course of that marriage the husband was employed at all times by the same company and is due to retire a year from now, does the wife have some interest in his pension? The general answer to that question is yes. Does that mean that she gets one half of all his pension payments? That again is governed strictly by state law, but the general factors that will be looked at are how many of the pension eligibility years coincided with the years of the marriage, the actual contribution of each party to that marital asset, and to what extent were premarital assets utilized to acquire what now is deemed to be a marital asset.

Prenuptial and Property Settlement Agreements

Frequently, parties avoid court involvement in distribution of property by entering into a *prenuptial agreement* prior to the marriage or by entering into a *property settlement agreement* after the parties have agreed to separate. A *prenuptial agreement* is an agreement that sets forth, prior to the marriage, what the entitlement will be of either party in the marital estate in the event of a divorce. These types of agreements are becoming more and more common, especially in second marriages.

A *property settlement agreement* is an agreement or a contract entered into by a husband and wife after they have agreed to separate that sets forth the terms of any property distribution, custody arrangement, and support obligations.

Chapter Fifteen

Landlord/Tenant Rights

The relationship between a landlord and a tenant is governed by a contract. That contract is referred to as the *lease*. A *lease* is an agreement between the landlord and the tenant in which the landlord agrees to allow the tenant to occupy a building or a piece of property owned by the landlord generally in return for the payment of periodic rent. Any issues relating to landlord/tenant law must initially be looked at in terms of what the lease calls for as to the respective rights and obligations of the two parties.

It's the Law
Specific terms of the lease may be superseded by either local, state, or federal law.

The specific terms of the lease may be superseded by either local, state, or federal law. Federal law only comes into play regarding discrimination. The federal housing laws are designed to provide housing to all people without regard to classification. Many local and state governments have enacted landlord/tenant legislation. (Landlord/tenant laws normally only apply to residential leases.)

A *residential lease* is a lease between a landlord and an individual who intends to occupy that space as his or her residence. A *commercial lease*, on the other hand, is a lease between a landlord and a tenant who occupies the space for business or commercial reasons.

Landlord/tenant laws may come in a variety of different forms involving things such as rent control, the obligation of the landlord in dealing with security deposits, the obligations of the landlord to maintain the premises in a habitable condition, and a multitude of other such issues. A frequent source of controversy between landlord and tenant is the return of the security deposit at the end of the lease. Either state or local law or the lease itself governs how the security deposit is handled.

In order to fully ascertain the respective rights and obligations of the parties to a lease, you must first look at the lease itself and then determine whether there are any local or state statutory provisions that may override or supersede any provisions within the lease. For instance, if a landlord, in renewing a residential lease, chooses to increase the rent, but the pertinent rent control law precludes such an increase in rent, that law will supersede the terms of the lease. The landlord can obtain no more rent than what the law allows, even if agreed to by the tenant.

Likewise, if the lease provides that the landlord is not responsible for maintenance of the premises, that too may be superseded by the landlord/tenant law that applies in that jurisdiction. It may expressly impose the obligation upon the landlord to maintain the entire premises in a reasonably habitable condition. Indeed many such landlord/tenant laws not only impose that obligation on the landlord, but also give the tenant the right to *abate* or reduce the rent if the tenant has to incur expenses in order to make the premises reasonably habitable.

Evictions of tenants by landlords are a frequent source of litigation. In residential leases, a landlord is generally barred from evicting a tenant without first obtaining a court order. The purpose of requiring the court's involvement is to provide some degree of neutrality and oversight of the eviction process so that the landlord does not wrongfully evict the tenant.

The scope of the law governing the landlord/tenant relationship may be further expanded by case law interpreting the landlord/tenant law of that jurisdiction.

Leases

A *lease*, being a contract, is subject to all of the comments made previously in the section on contracts. In addition, there are several provisions within a lease that both parties need to be sensitive to.

◆ *Destruction*. The lease will frequently set forth the rights of the tenant if the premises should be destroyed by fire or other catastrophe. A fairly typical provision would be to allow the tenant to declare the lease null and void if the premises cannot be restored to its prior condition within sixty days. Obviously the tenant does not have to pay rent during the period of time when the premises are not habitable. Such a provision, however, may be highly detrimental to the tenant because it may obligate him or her to occupy the premises on the sixtieth day assuming it is restored to habitable condition. (That is not much solace to the tenant if he or she has no place to live or to run his or her business during this sixty day period.)

◆ *Subletting*. Frequently a lease will bar subletting. This may be important from the landlord's point of view because the general rule of law is that any contract (including a lease) can be assigned unless there is a provision within the contract that says it cannot be assigned. An *assignment* simply means that one party to the contract may assign or sell his or her rights to a third person. In the case of a tenant, the subletting of the premises is an assignment of the tenant's rights to a third person who would then have the right to occupy the premises in lieu of the tenant who signed the lease. However, if the lease precludes that, then subletting may be prohibited. (From a landlord's point of view such a prohibition is desirable because the landlord wants to know with whom he or she is dealing.)

◆ *Uses*. The lease should expressly state what the tenant's intended uses of the premises are and confirm that these uses do not in any way violate any condominium association regulations, homeowner's association regulations, or zoning regulations.

◆ *Taxes, utilities, insurance, and condo fees*. The lease should indicate who is responsible for payment of these.

◆ *Security deposit*. The lease should expressly indicate what the amount of the security deposit is, who is holding it, whether it is being held in an interest-bearing account, and how much time the landlord has after the termination of the lease to make an accounting for and return of the security deposit.

◆ *Obligations and rights of the parties.* The lease should indicate exactly what the respective obligations and rights are of the landlord and the tenant. Things that should be addressed are the landlord's right of access, the tenant's right to make alterations, the need for smoke detectors or carbon monoxide detectors, and the use of any heavy equipment or electrical items that may overload the system.

◆ *Subordination.* If the owner of the property is liable on a mortgage or deed of trust as to the property, then it is prudent for the owner to state in the lease that the lease is subject and subordinate to all mortgages and deeds of trust. Most leases will also state that the tenant agrees to sign all documents upon the request of the landlord confirming subordination or in the alternative the landlord is authorized to sign such documents on behalf of the tenant. (This issue would only come into play if the premises were going to be refinanced or sold and the lender required some confirmation that, in the event of a foreclosure, its right to foreclose would not be impeded by the existence of tenants on the premises.)

◆ *Joint liability.* If there are two or more tenants on the lease, then the lease may expressly state that the tenants are *jointly and severally liable.* That means if there is a default or a breach by the tenants, the landlord can collect 100% of the money due on the lease from either one or both of the tenants. (That provision works to the landlord's advantage because it allows the landlord to collect 100% of the lease payment from either tenant.)

◆ *Personal guarantee.* If the lease is in the name of a business entity, frequently the landlord will require a guarantee of the person who owns or manages that business entity. (That obligates that person on the lease as if he or she were named as a tenant.)

Chapter Sixteen

Estates and Probate

The law dealing with estates governs the passing of the property of people who have passed away as well as people who during their life either voluntarily or involuntarily have conveyed their property to a third person for purposes of managing that property.

Probating a Will

The law dealing with decedents is sometimes referred to as probate. The term *probate* literally means "to prove." What is proved in this instance is a *will*. A will is a written statement signed by a person expressly indicating his or her wishes regarding the disposition of his or her assets at death. A will never becomes an operative document until that person passes away. Prior to the person's death, the will may be amended at any time assuming that the person is competent. That amendment is called a *codicil*.

Some states allow handwritten or *holographic wills*. A holographic will must be completely in the handwriting of the person signing the will. That is, you cannot have someone else handwrite a will for you. If there are any words on the will other than your own, the will may be considered ineffective. The problem with a handwritten will is that it is not *self-proving* or *self-authenticating*. The executor would need to bring witnesses to the courthouse to prove that it is authentic.

The validity of a will may be challenged for a number of reasons. The most common challenges are fraud, undue influence, or duress. All these concepts have been addressed in Chapter 12 and those comments have equal application here.

The objective of a will is to provide for an orderly transfer of assets from one generation to the next. If a person dies without a will, then the transfer of his or her assets will be governed by the *law of intestacy*. The law of intestacy is that body of law established in the state code that dictates who will be the recipient or recipients of the decedent's property if the decedent dies without a will. It always is preferable to have a will since that gives you control over how your property will pass. If you do not have a will, then the law of intestacy rules. That law varies dramatically from state to state, but typically it establishes an order of priority in which most of the assets go to the surviving spouse. If there is no surviving spouse, the assets normally go to the surviving children, and if there are no surviving children, then perhaps to parents or siblings of the decedent.

If a person dies with a will, that will should be probated. *Probating the will* simply means presenting the will to the clerk of the local court that has jurisdiction over wills and estates and proving that it is authentic. Most wills are self-authenticating. That means they are witnessed by the number of persons required by state law, notarized, and contain the necessary language required by state law in order to make them self-proving or self-authenticating. If the will is self-proving or self-authenticating, then all that needs to be done is for the executor to present the will to the clerk of the court. The clerk will then accept it upon payment of the proper filing fee.

Executor

Normally, in a will, there is a designation of an *executor*. The role of the executor is to gather all the assets of the decedent, report to the court what those assets are, and then supervise the orderly distribution of those assets in accordance with the will. If a person dies without a will, then the individual that is appointed for this purpose normally is referred to as an *administrator*. An administrator and serves the same general function as an executor.

The process of gathering the assets, reporting to the court, and then distributing the assets is supervised by the local court where the will was probated. Generally there is a court officer who is responsible for that supervision. The purpose of court supervision is to ensure that the wishes of the decedent are carried out.

The administration of estates can sometimes take many years depending upon the size and complexity of the estate and the terms of the will, including the administration of any trusts created by the will. As part of the administration of an estate, any potential creditors should be given notice of the fact that the estate is being administered. Those creditors then have a designated period of time to make claims against the estate. If those claims are not made within the time allowed, they are deemed to be denied. At that point, the assets of the estate can be distributed after payment of all lawful debts of the estate.

Taxes

In the administration of any estate, there may be significant tax consequences. An estate that consists simply of a marital transfer—from one spouse to another—normally does not involve any estate tax consequences. Instead, the tax consequences will occur when that surviving spouse passes away. The objective of this tax law provision is to attempt to ensure that the surviving spouse has sufficient assets during his or her life to maintain him- or herself, but then upon the death of the surviving spouse the estate will be taxed according to the federal estate tax law. There may, however, be state inheritance taxes that must be considered.

Taxation of property transferred by an individual to others at his or her death is one of the oldest and most common forms of taxation. Gift taxes and death taxes in the form of estate or inheritance taxes are generally referred to as *transfer taxes*. The transfer of property may be in the form of a gift or in the form of a conveyance at the time of death. A federal tax on transfers at death was first employed in the form of an inheritance tax in 1862. At first it applied only to personal property, but later it was extended to real property as well. In order to avoid the federal and state taxes on transfer of property at death, some property owners made large transfers during their life. To counteract this technique (and partly for political reasons) the *Federal Gift Tax* was enacted in 1924.

The transfer taxes were not enacted merely to raise revenue. In fact, they do not raise much revenue compared to other federal taxes. In part they were designed to prevent people from accumulating large blocks of wealth and then transmitting those blocks from generation to generation. Overall the IRS has not been terribly successful in that regard.

In determining federal estate tax liability, the first issue that must be addressed is the *gross estate*. The gross estate includes, at a minimum, the value of all property owned by the decedent at death that passes to somebody else. This includes some life insurance proceeds and some jointly owned property. The gross estate for tax purposes is not necessarily the same as the estate that might be reported to the local court for probate purposes.

Once the gross estate has been calculated, there are certain allowable deductions that may be taken to arrive at what is referred to as the taxable estate. Those deductions include allowances for most transfers to a surviving spouse (the marital deduction), contributions to charity, and deductions for certain debts and expenses.

The gift tax is designed to be a companion tax to the estate tax. The gift tax applies to any gratuitous transmission of property during a person's life since a transfer of that nature has the effect of reducing the estate subject to estate tax at the time of death. There are certain exclusions in regard to the gift tax. For instance, each year a person is entitled to an annual exclusion for gifts in an amount of $11,000 to each donee. Only if the amount given is more than that excludable amount in one year to one donee will the gift be taxable.

> ### It's the Law
> *The gross estate for tax purposes is not necessarily the same as for probate purposes.*

Generally, the property transferred from one spouse to another at the time of death is not subject to any estate tax. If the surviving spouse consumes part of what he or she inherited and holds at the time of his or her death an amount less than the estate tax exemption, then he or she will be able to transmit that property outright without a tax on his or her estate because the exemption would apply to that. That exempt amount increases from year to year. As of 2009, it is $3,500,000.

It makes sense to take advantage of that exemption in most instances for each party. In order to do that, each party would have to have an estate at the time of death of as much as the exempt amount. That can be done by means of establishing a marital trust.

Example: *Suppose that the total estate of a couple is over the exempt amount. Also suppose that the husband passes away first and a marital trust has been established for the benefit of the wife. The exempt amount would pass to the wife at the time of the husband's death outright. The remaining money would be in trust that could be used for her benefit under the terms of the trust at the passing of the husband. The money that was held in trust would then pass to the next generation free of estate tax.*

If on the other hand the entire estate had passed to the wife at the time of death and assuming that she did not consume any portion of that, then her estate would be subject to tax on the amount over the exempt amount.

A few important things to remember about federal transfer taxes are the following.

◆ Estates valued in 2004 at under $1,500,000 are not subject to any taxation. The valuation of an estate, however, includes not just assets and properties in existence at the time of death, but also the entitlement to certain life insurance proceeds. For the years 2005 through 2009, estates must be valued at or above the figures listed below, otherwise they are not subject to taxation under the Federal Estate Tax:

2005—$1,500,000
2006— $2,000,000
2007— $2,000,000
2008— $2,000,000
2009— $3,500,000

In the year 2010, the *Federal Estate Tax* may come back in the same form as how it existed before the statutory amendments—unless Congress decides otherwise.

◆ Assets that are simply transferred from one spouse to another are not subject to federal estate tax at the time of the death of the first spouse. At the death of the second spouse, they become subject to taxation. There are a number of ways in which the estate tax burden can be reduced because of that fact. The principal mechanism is the *marital estate trust*.

Guardianship, Power of Attorney, and Trust

A second component of estate law deals with transfers of property either voluntarily or involuntarily from one person to another during that person's life. Such a transfer may come in the form of a *trust* or *guardianship* (*conservatorship*). A guardianship is normally established when a person is considered to be incompetent to manage his or her own personal financial affairs and therefore needs to have a guardian appointed to manage those affairs. In such a proceeding, the local court first determines the person to be incompetent or otherwise incapacitated, and then designates a *guardian* or *conservator* to manage that person's estate and perhaps also to manage that person's life. The guardian then becomes the decision-maker for that person in all aspects as allowed by the court order.

If the court order authorizes the guardian to completely control the assets of that person, then those assets are to be managed in the method deemed best by the guardian. The guardian must act in the best interest of the person who has been declared incapacitated (the *ward* or the *beneficiary*), and the guardian must report to the court on a periodic basis as to where the assets are, to what extent they have been expended, and what they have been expended for. A frequent instance in which you see a guardianship created is when a parent becomes too elderly or infirm to manage his or her own affairs. In that event, the children may request the court to have a guardian appointed who will then manage the parent's financial and personal affairs.

Another way to accomplish this same objective of guardianship is through a *durable power of attorney*. A *power of attorney* is a document wherein one person authorizes another person to act in his or her behalf either generally or for a specific purpose. The durable power of attorney is a document signed by the person whose assets are to be managed that expressly states that the power of attorney shall continue in the event of the disability of the signator. That durable power of attorney then continues in existence after a person becomes incompetent.

It's the Law

A power of attorney authorizes another person to act on your behalf.

For instance, a spouse who is about to go into serious surgery may sign a durable power of attorney to the other spouse, authorizing the other spouse to sign his or her name to checks, to convey real estate, and to do all acts that the first spouse could do if he or she was fully competent.

The advantage of a durable power of attorney is that it is less formal than a guardianship. The disadvantage of a durable power of attorney is that it does not involve court supervision and therefore creates potential for abuse on the part of the attorney or the person in control.

Another type of conveyance that may be subject to court supervision is a trust. A trust, very simply, is an agreement, normally in writing, wherein one person (the trustor) conveys property to another person (the trustee) for the benefit of a beneficiary. The *trustor* and the *beneficiary* may be one and the same person. For instance, you may convey property to your wife in trust for her to use for your benefit in the event you become incompetent and cannot manage your own affairs. In doing so, you have actually conveyed that property to your wife, making her the *legal* owner of the property, *but* she can only use it for your benefit. On your death, the trust assets would go to the beneficiaries designated in the trust.

A trust may be filed with the local court in some areas. If filed, it then becomes subject to court supervision much like a guardianship. On the other hand, a trust not filed acts very similarly to a power of attorney, in that there is no court supervision of how the assets are managed.

Living Will and Advance Medical Directive

If you have ever been admitted to a hospital for any reason, then you have probably been asked by the hospital personnel whether you have a *living will* or an *advance medical directive*. The terms are somewhat different in different states, but their objective is much the same—to provide some advance direction to your survivors as to what your wishes are in the event that you pass into a coma or are otherwise unable to give direction as to future medical care.

In such instruments, you designate an *agent* who can make those decisions for you, typically after it has been determined by two doctors (or one doctor and a licensed clinical psychologist) that it is unlikely that you will regain consciousness or any meaningful form of life within a prescribed period. These documents are very powerful because they place a great deal of trust in the person that you designate as your agent.

Chapter Seventeen

Taxes

Taxes are something that everyone is familiar with. You can be taxed at the federal level, state level, and local level. Federal tax consists mostly of income taxes and estate taxes. At the state level, taxes may come in the form of income tax, sales tax, inheritance tax, and licensing taxes. At the local level, typically the taxes are licensing taxes and personal property taxes, although some localities may have the authority to impose income taxes and sales taxes. (The complexity of the tax laws throughout the nation far exceeds the scope of this book.)

Taxes are generally thought of as a means for the government to generate funding for its operations. Taxes, however, are strongly rooted in social policy. If the sole purpose of taxes was simply to generate money to support the government, then a flat tax on income would make perfect sense. A flat tax of perhaps 17% on all income would be simple for the taxpayer and also easy for the government to administer.

The concept of flat tax makes a lot of sense. Unfortunately, it does not pass muster in the face of political reality. The governmental taxing authority has never been used solely for the purpose of raising money. Governmental taxing authority also reflects social policy. Through the tax code, the government intends to promote a number of things such as energy conservation, home ownership, family life, etc. As such, the likelihood of the federal government ever imposing a flat tax for income purposes is slight.

It's the Law
Governmental taxing authority reflects social policy.

Federal Taxes

At the federal level, the primary tax is the *income tax*. Most know this form of taxation by the completion of the annual 1040 form for the IRS. The income tax is a relatively new creation, having only been in existence for approximately a hundred years. The income tax is designed to tax anything that is referred to as income or what otherwise might be thought of as *economic gain*. That gain can come in the form of wages, profits from the sale of property and securities, earnings from gambling, or proceeds from winning the lottery.

If you buy stock at $100 per share and sell it at $300 per share, then your profit of $200 per share is subject to taxation. The amount of tax that you will pay depends in part whether it is subject to long- or short-term capital gains. *Long-term capital gains* are gains that relate to property you have held for more than twelve months (generally), and are subject to a lower tax than short-term capital gains or profits.

Overall, the amount of tax that you pay depends upon what *tax bracket* you are in. Currently there are several different tax brackets that are governed by your overall income level.

Whatever income you have may be subject to certain deductions and also to a variety of different credits that may be available. A *deduction* reduces your adjusted gross income. Common deductions are the home mortgage interest deduction, the payment of state taxes, the payment of real estate taxes, and charitable deductions. These deductions do not reduce your tax burden dollar-for-dollar. Instead, they simply reduce the amount of income you have that is subject to tax at whatever your tax rate may be.

Deductions are contrasted with *tax credits*. A *tax credit* is a dollar-for-dollar reduction of your tax obligation. For instance, if your adjusted gross income is $100,000 and your total deductions are $40,000, then your taxable income is $60,000. At that level of income, your total obligation may be in the range of $20,000. If you then have credits that you are entitled to, those credits will reduce that $20,000 obligation dollar-for-dollar. As such, if you have the entitlement to $5,000 in credits, then your actual tax burden will only be $15,000.

Income that you receive in some instances can be subject to *double taxation*. For instance, if you are a principal owner of a corporation and the corporation receives income, then the corporation may be taxed on that income. If you then distribute that income to yourself as compensation for being an officer or as shareholder dividends, then that income may be taxed a second time as your personal income. This double taxation can be avoided by designating your corporation as an *S corporation*. In an *S corporation* this tax liability is passed through to the individual owner or owners. In a *C corporation* the tax liability may exist both at the corporate level and at the individual level for the individual owners.

Another federal tax is the *Federal Estate and Gift Tax*. This form of taxation is discussed in Chapter 16, dealing with estates.

State Taxes

At the state level, taxes may come in several different forms. The state income tax that exists in most states is generally keyed to the federal income tax, in which information from your federal return is transferred directly to your state return forms. The tax at the state level for income is generally considerably less than at the federal level.

Other forms of state taxes include the sales tax, which is a tax on the sale of all goods. The *sales tax* is sometimes referred to as a *regressive tax*, meaning that it taxes lower income people disproportionately. That is, a 4% tax on sales of food and other necessities to someone earning $200,000 per year may not be a big bite on their budget, but a 4% tax on these sales for someone earning $20,000 is a big bite.

There may also be a number of different state licensing taxes. Those taxes may come in the form of licensing *motor vehicles*, *professional licenses*, or *occupational licenses*. Many localities have what is referred to as a *business license tax*. This tax in some jurisdictions is called a *gross receipts tax*. Generally, the rate for this tax is fairly low, but it is a tax on essentially every dollar that business brings in the door, irrespective of how much actual income the owner of the business may derive from it. As such, a business may have gross receipts of $1,000,000 and also have expenses of $1,000,000, in which event there is no income generated. That business, however, is still going to pay a gross receipts tax on the $1,000,000 of gross receipts.

IRS

The Internal Revenue Service (IRS) is an agency within the Department of the Treasury. The main office of the Internal Revenue Service is in Washington, D.C. The regional offices are divided into seven geographic areas. In each region there are ten service centers that primarily deal with the processing of returns, selections for audit, and in-office audits.

In 1988, Congress passed a taxpayer's bill of rights. This bill of rights requires that the IRS inform the taxpayer regarding the determination or collection of tax in simple and nontechnical terms. Taxpayers are also entitled to notice regarding the procedures for appealing adverse decisions, prosecuting refund claims, and filing taxpayer complaints. In addition, the IRS must notify the taxpayer of collection and enforcement procedures under the Internal Revenue Code.

A return filed with the Internal Revenue Service may be examined closely or not at all. In most cases, the review of the return at the service center is the beginning and the end of the Internal Revenue Service review. Some returns, however, are sent for further examination. A small minority of those returns are then subjected to an *audit*. If the taxpayer disputes the initial determination of liability in the audit process, the taxpayer may appeal that decision within the Internal Revenue Service.

The theory behind auditing tax returns is to encourage taxpayers to comply voluntarily with the tax laws. The selection of returns for review involves both computer analysis and also a manual inspection of the returns. What the IRS looks for in those returns is a high probability of error resulting in some significant change in tax owed. These audits may be conducted at the service center or more significant audits may be conducted at the district office.

An audit at the district office level may consist of an office audit that is performed by tax auditors in an IRS office or it may consist of a field audit, which involves the examining agent making an appointment at a time and place convenient to the taxpayer. At any such audit, the taxpayer has a right to have his or her accountant or attorney present. The possible outcomes of an audit are:

- no change in the tax owed;
- a proposed adjustment with the taxpayer signing a waiver of notice of any deficiency; or,
- a proposed adjustment with the taxpayer refusing to accept any adjustments proposed by the auditor.

In contested cases, the taxpayer will receive a thirty-day letter. This letter entitles the taxpayer to file a written protest to the proposed adjustments to the tax owed. If the taxpayer does not respond to the thirty-day letter, then the IRS will attempt to contact the taxpayer regarding his or her choice of action. If there is no response from the taxpayer then the IRS issues a ninety-day letter called a Notice of Deficiency.

If the taxpayer chooses to protest after receipt of the thirty-day letter, then the matter may be reviewed by the appeals office within the Internal Revenue Service. If the taxpayer wishes to pursue the matter further, he or she must take the case to court. Taking a tax case to court means filing a petition before the Tax Court of the United States or filing suit in the United States District Court in the district where the taxpayer resides or with the United States Court of Claims in Washington, D.C.

Before the United States District Court acquires jurisdiction over such a claim, the deficiency in taxes must be paid by the taxpayer. This is an important distinction between actions filed in the U.S. District Court versus actions filed in the Tax Court. A tax case filed in the U.S. Tax Court does not require the taxpayer to pay the deficiency before filing the suit. There may be other tactical advantages in filing in one court versus the other depending on which federal district you live in and the current tax policies at that time in the Tax Court or Court of Claims.

Chapter Eighteen

Real Estate

Real estate law to some extent is similar to contract law in that the underpinning of most real estate transactions is a contract. A contract to sell real estate is an agreement between a buyer and a seller to convey title to a piece of real estate for a given price. What is meant by *title* to real estate is the name of the persons or entities identified as the owner on the legal document known as a *deed*. Those persons are identified as being the *title* or the *legal owners* of the property.

Other persons may have an *equitable interest* in the property. What that means is that before the property can be sold, those equitable interests or claims would have to be satisfied. For instance, a lender, lien holders, or perhaps a spouse whose name is not on the deed may as a matter of law have an equitable interest in the property.

A contract for sale of real estate may contain a number of contingencies. A *contingency* is a provision within the contract that states that the contract may be declared null and void by one or both parties unless certain events occur. For instance, a standard provision within a commercial real estate contract is what is known as a *feasibility contingency*. The feasibility contingency generally gives the purchaser anywhere from thirty to sixty days to study the property to determine whether it can be used for the commercial purpose for which the buyer intends to use it. The study by the purchaser may involve a review of the zoning laws, studies of the soil to make sure that the land is suitable for the intended construction, or engineering analyses to determine that the contour of the land is appropriate for the intended construction.

A similar type of contingency is found in a residential contract. It is generally referred to as a *home inspection contingency*. A home inspection contingency usually gives the purchaser anywhere from five to ten days to have the home inspected to determine whether it meets with the purchaser's approval. At any time during the home inspection contingency, the purchaser may rescind the contract.

Another contingency within most contracts is the *finance contingency*. That is, the buyer's obligation to settle is contingent upon the buyer being able to get the necessary financing or money from a lender on terms agreeable to the buyer in order to acquire the property. If the buyer cannot do that, then the buyer's obligation to settle on the contract is nullified. Once all of the contingencies have been removed, the buyer and the seller are irrevocably locked into going to settlement.

A real estate settlement typically consists of the parties appearing either at a lawyer's office or the office of a settlement agent. There the seller signs a deed to the property. The purchaser signs whatever financing documents are necessary to obtain the loan. Then, a variety of other documents may be signed in order to satisfy the requirements of the institutional lender who provides the money for the purchase of the property and the title insurance company who insures that good and marketable title passes to the buyer.

In going to *settlement* or *closing* (the terms are generally used synonymously), title to the property is conveyed from a seller to a purchaser. The conveyance of title is accomplished by a document referred to as a deed. A deed is a written instrument signed by the seller, identifying the property in question by precise legal description, and stating the nature of the title interest being conveyed by the seller to the purchaser.

The deed may then be recorded at the courthouse to serve as a notification to the entire world that the seller is no longer the owner of this property but on the date in question has conveyed the property to the purchaser. The conveyance is considered to be effective when the deed is physically delivered by the seller to the purchaser. The delivery normally occurs at settlement when the seller signs the deed and then tenders it to the settlement agent who acts on behalf of the purchaser.

There are a number of different forms of title ownership that may be conveyed. The most common forms of title ownership are referred to as legal title and equitable title. *Legal title* is determined by looking at the deed to determine who at that point in time is recognized by the deed as the owner of the property. *Equitable title* refers to the interest another person or institution, such as a bank, may have in a piece of property.

Example: *Harry and Wilma purchased a piece of property twenty years ago. When they bought the property, there was a deed conveying the property to them. They are the title owners of that piece of property. They have never sold that property to anyone else. They have, however, conveyed equitable title to the lender who initially loaned them the money to purchase the property. They have also refinanced the property several times and therefore have signed additional documents conveying equitable title to those subsequent lenders.*

Different jurisdictions handle real estate financing in different ways. In some states, the real estate financing that is utilized for a purchaser to buy real estate is a *mortgage*. In other instances, it may be a *deed of trust*. Although those different documents can have significantly different meanings, the effect is much the same—giving a security interest in your real estate to the lender who loaned you the money in order to acquire the property or to refinance the property.

If you do not make your monthly payments in a timely fashion, the lender may decide to *foreclose*. If they foreclose, that means they are going to sell your property at a public auction where anyone could come in and bid on your property. The objective of the lender in that instance is to recover all of the money loaned to you that is still outstanding, plus any interest that is due at that point, along with any expenses, trustee fees, and/or attorney's fees that they have incurred in having to foreclose.

Example: *Suppose you buy a piece of property for $100,000 and you obtain 90% financing (meaning that 90% of the purchase price is coming from a lender). That means that you would have to put $10,000 of your own money into the purchase in order to go to settlement. At settlement, you will receive a deed from the seller indicating that legal title is being conveyed to you. At settlement, you would also sign a mortgage or deed of trust wherein you are conveying equitable title to the lender to secure the $90,000 loan.*

Under the terms of that document, the lender gives you the right to remain in the property and to treat it as your home, but in return you have to make sure that you properly insure the property, properly maintain it, and most importantly, make the monthly payments on time. If you fail to do those things, then the lender can foreclose and attempt to sell the property in order to recoup the $90,000 and outstanding interest that may still be due, plus any additional cost or expenses that they have incurred.

If that property were to go to foreclosure and were to be sold at a public auction shortly after you acquire the property, then it is unlikely that the lender would be able to sell the property for much more than what you paid for it and, as such, there probably would be no surplus or excess left in the sale price that would go back to you.

Determining Title

Sometimes, in the course of dealing with a piece of real estate, there may arise an issue of who owns it. Every state has its own way of recording ownership interest in real estate. One way of determining the owner of a piece of real estate is to call the local real estate tax office. The tax office should have a record of who they report as being the owner of the real estate. Those records are, however, not always reliable. In order to determine the true owner or owners of a piece of real estate you may need to have a title search done. There are *title examiners* or *title insurance companies* that are available to do that for a fee. That is probably the only sure way to determine who all of the owners are of a piece of real estate as of a specific date.

A title examiner, in determining ownership interest, will check all of the various indices at the local courthouse (or other governmental office building where deeds and land records are maintained) to determine who the last person to have been deeded that property was. This may tell you who the title owner of the real estate is as of that date, but it does not tell you whether there could be any other persons that might have a right to claim some interest in that property. As such it may be necessary to do a *historical search* of the chain of title going back many years to determine who all the other title owners had been.

To do a thorough search of the title, it would be necessary to determine whether during the ownership interest of any of the title owners there had been any *liens* noted of record that might apply to the property. Liens may come in the form of *tax liens, mortgage liens, deeds of trust, mechanics liens*, or *judgment liens*. If there have been any such liens, it must be determined whether those liens have been properly released so that they no longer apply to the property.

If any of the title owners passed away during the period of their ownership of the property, it may be necessary to check the will index to determine whether their will is of record. If it is, then their will must be examined for what it indicates as far as the transfer of this property. If there is no will, additional searches at the courthouse or recorder's office will be necessary.

Suffice it to say that in many states the determination of the true owners of a piece of property can be very complex. If you are simply interested in general information as to ownership interest, reliance upon the tax records may be sufficient. If, however, you are contemplating purchasing real estate or filing a legal action against the property owners, it is advisable to have an appropriate title search done of the property to make sure you are acquiring good title or suing the correct owners.

> ## It's the Law
> *The determination of the true owners of a piece of property can be very complex.*

Adverse Possession

As indicated, the traditional way by which a person acquires ownership of a piece of property is by means of a deed. There is a principle recognized in real estate law known as *adverse possession,* which is another means by which a person may acquire ownership of a piece of property.

Example: *You decide that you would like to use the small lot next to your home to park your boat. You know the lot is owned by your next door neighbor. You park your boat on that property and use and maintain that piece of property for your own purposes* freely, openly, *and* exclusively *over a period of time. By doing so, you may acquire adverse possession of that property.*

The period of time for which you must *adversely possess* the property is dictated by state law. Generally it takes from twenty to forty years. Once that period of time has passed and the true title owner has not objected to your use of the property, the law may deem you to be the owner of that property by adverse possession. In order to truly acquire title to that piece of property, however, a suit would have to be filed to have the court confirm that you acquired the property by means of adverse possession.

Real Estate Contracts

If you are contemplating entering into a real estate contract, you should have the contract reviewed by an attorney. All of the considerations previously mentioned regarding contracts would be applicable to a real estate contract. In addition, some specific things that you should be on the lookout for are the following.

Property Description

The property must be precisely described. There are different ways of describing a piece of real estate. It can be described by means of a street address. The street address for purposes of a residential contract may be sufficient. However, the so-called legal description should also be added. The legal description is the description as set forth in the deed by which the current owner acquired the property. That legal description may frequently be referenced by a subdivision with a section number and a lot number.

Another means of describing a piece of real estate is by means of a *tax number* or *tax map number*. Many jurisdictions have broken every piece of property down by number for purposes of taxing.

Another means of describing a piece of real estate is called a *metes and bounds* description. *Metes and bounds* is a description, generally given by a surveyor, wherein the surveyor describes the entire perimeter of the property in terms of distance and compass directions.

It is not unheard of that people enter into a real estate contract thinking that they are buying one piece of property and in fact they end up taking title to a different piece of property. If there is any doubt in your mind as to what piece of property you are buying, you need to have a survey done, and perhaps even meet with that surveyor at the property so that you can actually walk the property bounds.

Earnest Money Deposit

The *earnest money deposit* is an amount of money that literally is designed to show that the person making the offer to buy the property is *in earnest* about his or her intent to buy the property. If you make an offer to buy a piece of property for $1,000,000, but only propose an earnest money deposit of $100, that says that you are not truly in earnest. There is no strict requirement as to how much the earnest money deposit should be, but certainly it is not unusual that the earnest money be in the range of 5%–10% of the total contract price.

It must be clearly indicated how that earnest money deposit is going to be held. If it is going to be paid by means of check, then typically it would be tendered to a real estate broker that is involved in the transaction and then placed in that real estate broker's escrow account. If the contract is finally *ratified* (fully accepted), then the contract needs to state who gets the earnest money deposit in the event one or both parties defaults and fails to meet one or more of the contract terms. The earnest money deposit will be credited against the total price at settlement.

Financing

Most real estate purchases are going to be financed, generally by an *institutional lender*—a bank or mortgage company. *Financing terms* (the *amount* being financed, the *interest rate*, the *term of the note*, etc.) should be spelled out in the contract. From the purchaser's point of view, the contract should be contingent upon these terms so as to give the purchaser as much leverage as possible to get out of the contract if he or she does not obtain the financing that he or she is looking for.

If there is any financing that is being provided by the seller, then that likewise needs to be spelled out. For instance, if the property is being sold for $100,000 and the purchaser is obtaining $50,000 of that purchase price from a bank and the seller then is going to hold a *promissory note* for $50,000 for the balance of the purchase price then the specific terms for each should be spelled out in the contract. The bank's promissory note would likely be secured by a first deed of trust against the real estate and the seller's promissory note would then be secured by a second deed of trust. A promissory note is a document signed by a person or entity promising to pay money to another person or entity under certain terms (interest rate, due date, place of payment, means of payment, etc.).

Contingencies

In most real estate contracts there is a financing contingency. This means that the buyer's obligation to actually go to settlement is contingent upon the buyer obtaining financing (money for the purchase) from a lender on the terms specified in the contract. If the lender rejects the loan application of the buyer, the buyer usually cannot go to settlement. In a typical residential real estate contract, the buyer has to obtain a loan commitment from a lender prior to settlement and upon obtaining that loan commitment the financing contingency may be removed.

Removal of the financing contingency, however, is always somewhat dangerous because there are situations that could arise in which the buyer may not be able to get the financing from that lender. The buyer always wants to have a way of getting out of the contract in the event he or she cannot get the financing. The seller, on the other hand, would like to lock the buyer in by having that financing contingency removed at some point in time prior to settlement. Another type of contingency would be a feasibility or inspection contingency as previously mentioned.

Title to the Property

The contract must specify that the seller will give *good title* to the property. Title can be conveyed in different ways in different jurisdictions. Typically title is conveyed by a general *warranty deed*. This means that the seller represents that he or she has good title and that he or she is giving clear title to the buyer (with the only exceptions being anything that may be noted in the title insurance policy that the buyer has obtained).

Typically, a buyer must obtain a *title insurance policy* for the protection of the lender. A buyer may also purchase an owner's title insurance policy for his or her own benefit. Title insurance is designed to insure that any defects in title will be cleared by the title insurance company or the title insurance company will have to pay the buyer or lender for any costs incurred as a result of nondisclosed problems with the title. *Lender's* title insurance protects only the lender's interest in the property. *Owner's* title insurance provides broader protection and would cover the owner for *any* nonreported title problems that may arise with the property during the owner's ownership of the property. In most transactions, it makes sense for the purchasers to strongly consider purchasing an owner's title insurance policy.

Closing Costs and Taxes

The contract should set forth the various closing costs that may be associated with the transaction and whether they are to be paid by the purchaser or the seller. Real estate property taxes should be the responsibility of the person who holds title up to the date of closing and thereafter will be the responsibility of the purchaser. In some instances there may be what are known as *roll back taxes* that could come into play once the property is sold. The contract needs to address who is responsible for those. Roll back taxes most often apply to rural property where tax has been deferred to promote farming of the property.

Personal Property, Fixtures, or Equipment

If there is any personal property, mechanical equipment, or other fixtures or furniture that are conveyed as part of the transaction, the contract should indicate that all those items will be conveyed in the same condition that they were in as of the date the contract was signed.

Ratification

The contract should expressly indicate what the *date of ratification* is. The date of ratification is the date that all offers, counteroffers, and counter demands must either be accepted or rejected—it is the date upon which the parties must come to a complete agreement on all the issues addressed in the written contract. The date of ratification is important because any contingency periods or other dates set forth in the contract will flow from that date. There should be a statement at the end of the contract expressly stating the date of ratification.

Representations of Seller and Buyer

If there are any representations being made either by the seller or the buyer, those should be set forth in the contract. Typical representations made by the seller are that he or she has good title, that there are no pending suits or actions that might impede or adversely affect the sale of the property, that there is no pending bankruptcy, that sale of the property will not result in any breach or default on his or her part, and that there are no hazardous substances on the property. A typical representation by the purchaser is that if the purchaser acts on behalf of a corporation or partnership that he or she has full authority to purchase the property and to sign the contract.

Risk of Loss

This is an important provision in any contract dealing with real estate that has structures on it. Once a contract has been ratified for the sale of real estate, the risk of loss may shift to the buyer. If the structure on that piece of real estate burns down then it is the buyer's loss at that time, even though he or she has not actually gone to settlement on the piece of property. Therefore it is important that the contract expressly state the risk of loss does not pass to the buyer until the date of closing.

Real Estate Commissions

If there are any real estate agents involved, it must be expressly stated who the agents are and what their commissions are. If either party has signed a listing agreement or a buyer-broker agreement, then the mere reference to such a document may suffice. If there are no real estate agents involved, that likewise should be expressly stated.

Attorney's Fees

Payment of attorney's fees and costs should be addressed in the event there is a breach or default by either party. That is, if litigation results, then it should be stated whether the prevailing party would be entitled to his or her attorney's fees and costs.

Disclosures

Under federal law, if a property has lead paint, then that must be disclosed. Under state law, it may be necessary to disclose or disclaim any defects in the property. If the property is a condominium or part of a homeowner's association, then state law may require that the documents of that condominium or homeowner's association be provided to the purchaser before the contract can become effective. Those documents may contain a variety of restrictions on the use of the property.

Chapter Nineteen

Business Organization

A business may be conducted in a number of different forms. Those forms consist of a *sole proprietorship*, a *partnership*, a *limited partnership*, a *corporation*, or a *limited liability company.*

Sole Proprietorships

A sole proprietorship is a business that is owned by a single individual. If I operate my business simply in the name of Brien A. Roche, Attorney at Law, then that is a sole proprietorship. A sole proprietorship is an individual conducting business in his or her own name or under a trade name.

A *trade name* is sometimes called a *fictitious name*. It is simply a name which a person or entity uses that is different than his or her legal name. For instance, if Todd Brown owns a trucking business under the name Todd's Truckers, then the trade name is Todd's Truckers. A sole proprietorship may have employees and may have several different business locations, but the entire business is owned by a single individual.

Partnerships

A partnership, on the other hand, is a joint venture of two or more people in which there is a sharing of both profits and losses. Partnerships can come in different forms. The two most common forms are general partnerships and limited partnerships. A *general partnership* exists when all of the partners share in profits and liabilities of the partnership. This does not necessarily mean that the sharing is equal. The sharing of profits and liabilities may be governed by the partnership agreement that the parties have entered into.

A *limited partnership*, on the other hand, is a legal entity in which there typically is only one general partner and there may be a number of limited partners. Those limited partners are much like investors or stockholders in a corporation. The limited partners normally have no control over the operation of the partnership and also normally have no liability for the acts of the partnership. They have simply contributed funds as an investment in the partnership and then expect to receive some return on their investment when the partnership begins to make money. Typically the sole rights of a limited partner are to share in the profits according to their partnership agreement.

Corporations

A corporation is a legal entity recognized by state or federal law and created under that law. A corporation can be formed by one or more individuals or by other business organizations. The principal benefits of a corporation are to shield those conducting the business from personal liability for the corporation's contractual obligations and to provide for the perpetual existence of the business.

Example: *The ABC Corporation enters into a lease with a landlord. If the ABC Corporation defaults on that lease, the landlord's claim for breach of the lease is against the ABC Corporation. It is not against those who own the corporation (unless the owners also signed the lease in their individual capacity).*

The shield from liability only applies to contract claims and not to personal tort claims.

Example: *Kelly is the owner of the ABC Corporation. While driving a company vehicle, she runs a red light and injures someone.*

She may be sued individually, along with her company known as the ABC Corporation.

However, if one of her employees is operating a company vehicle, runs a red light, and injures someone, then the parties who potentially may be liable as a result of that traffic accident are the employee who was driving and the ABC Corporation. Kelly, as the owner of the ABC Corporation, would not be personally liable.

There are instances in which corporate officers, directors, and controlling shareholders can be liable for tort actions of the corporation if they have implemented a policy that is deemed to be negligent.

Example: *Jeff, as president of a large delivery company, implements a policy requiring that all packages be delivered to the recipient within fifteen minutes of receipt by the delivery company. One of his drivers causes an accident because of this policy. At least under the law of some states, Jeff could be personally liable for that policy. He should know the policy is going to induce his employees to drive at a higher rate of speed in order to meet the time limitation, thereby causing some automobile accidents.*

A second benefit of a corporation is that a corporation has *perpetual existence*. That is, the corporation does not die when a shareholder or the president dies, but rather it continues to exist until it is terminated under the terms of the law under which it was created.

A corporation is formed by filing the appropriate documents with the state agency that supervises corporations. That document typically contains the name of the corporation, who the initial directors are, what the purpose of the corporation is, and the name and address of the registered agent who has been appointed by the corporation for the purpose of receiving important papers or legal documents.

Once a *corporate charter* has been approved by the governmental agency, it is necessary to have an organizational meeting of the corporation in which a board of directors is elected, officers are elected, and bylaws approved. If it is a stock corporation, typically shares of stock are issued at that time. Corporations may be privately held (privately held corporations are frequently referred to as *close corporations*) or it may be publicly held. A corporation that is publicly held is one that offers its shares of stock for purchase by members of the public. Many publicly traded corporations are on the various stock exchanges such as the New York Stock Exchange or the Nasdaq Exchange. (Not every publicly held corporation is listed on a stock exchange.)

As part of the organization of a corporation, *bylaws* are enacted by the board of directors. Bylaws are the constitution of the corporation that set forth the basic framework as to how the corporation will be operated. In addition, the shareholders may enter into a shareholder's agreement. A *shareholder's agreement* is a contract entered into between the shareholders in a privately held corporation that will govern their conduct in the event of the three Ds—death, disability, or deadlock. That is, the shareholder's agreement governs how the corporation is to be conducted and what will happen in the event that one of the shareholders dies, becomes disabled, or in the event that there is a deadlock between the shareholders. The shareholder's agreement may also govern a number of other rights between the shareholders.

> ## It's the Law
> *A shareholder's agreement governs in the event of the three Ds—death, disability, or deadlock.*

After a corporation has been duly formed, there may be periodic reporting requirements to the state in which the corporation has been formed. Those reporting requirements call for the corporation to report its current address, the name and address of its registered agent, and the name and address of its directors and/or officers.

As part of the start up of a corporation, a decision must be made as to whether the corporation should be an *S corporation* or a *C corporation*. (This issue was previously addressed in Chapter 17.)

A corporation may be terminated by filing a notice or articles of termination or dissolution with the appropriate agency. The mere fact that articles of termination or dissolution have been filed with the agency does not mean that the debts of that corporation evaporate. If the persons who control the corporation have raided the corporation and stripped it of its assets and thereby defrauded its creditors, then those individuals who are the owners may become personally liable for that fraudulent behavior.

Limited Liability Companies and Limited Liability Partnerships

Other forms of business organization are limited liability companies and limited liability partnerships. A *limited liability company (LLC)* is very similar to a corporation, but the reporting requirements to the state agency are generally less strenuous. The limitation on liability for an LLC is generally thought to be the same as a corporation. Limited liability companies have become quite popular over the last several years because they are easier to form than a corporation and involve fewer formalities in terms of paper work and reporting requirements to the state reporting agencies.

A *limited liability partnership* is a partnership wherein the partners are allowed to limit their particular liability for the conduct of other partners. One of the oddities of partnership law is that each general partner is liable for the conduct or misconduct of all other partners in the course of performing their partnership duties. Through a limited liability partnership, the partners can limit their liability.

Chapter Twenty

Bankruptcy

Years ago, the U.S. Congress felt that the issue of bankruptcy was sufficiently important that it needed to codify the law and thereby supplant any state laws that existed in regard to bankruptcy. This body of law has supplanted or replaced any state law, whether it be statutory or case law, dealing with issues of bankruptcy. You can find the Bankruptcy Code in the United States Code.

The general thrust of our bankruptcy laws is to provide protection to individuals or businesses who are in financial distress in order to either eventually give them a discharge from those financial obligations, or to give them some breathing room to be able to deal with their financial difficulties. It is hoped that they get back on their feet and are then able to repay their obligations either in whole or in part.

One of the main purposes of bankruptcy is to relieve an honest debtor of debts, thereby providing an opportunity for a fresh start. The bankruptcy laws also benefit creditors by providing a forum for either an orderly disposition of whatever assets a debtor may have or a plan for full or partial repayment of creditors. Creditors may be either secured or unsecured. A *secured creditor* may generally be thought of as someone that has a security interest or what might be referred to as a *lien interest* (such as a mortgage) against a piece of property. An *unsecured creditor* is someone like a credit card company or the telephone company that has no security to rely on.

In each federal district the Bankruptcy Court constitutes a unit of that U.S. District Court and receives its authority to hear cases and proceedings by referral from that U.S. District Court. Bankruptcy Court judges are appointed by the U.S. Courts of Appeals for that particular circuit to fourteen-year terms.

It's the Law

There are three basic types of bankruptcy filings—Chapter 7, Chapter 11, and Chapter 13.

There are three basic types of bankruptcy filings—Chapter 7 proceedings, Chapter 11 proceedings, and Chapter 13 proceedings. Chapter 7 cases may be thought of as *liquidation* proceedings in which the assets (if any) are liquidated (converted to cash) and used to satisfy creditors in the order of priority established. A Chapter 11 case is generally a *business reorganization* proceeding in which the debtor expects to continue operating. A *wage earner's proceeding* under Chapter 13 is designed to provide payment to creditors with the wage earner receiving an eventual discharge. Other differences between these three types are discussed later in the chapter.

Some basic principles that apply to all bankruptcy proceedings are the following.

- ◆ The *debtor* (the person filing the bankruptcy) is required by law to list all of his or her assets. If there is any hiding of assets, that may subject the debtor to criminal prosecution.
- ◆ The debtor must list all of his or her debts. Any debts that are not listed will not be discharged.
- ◆ Any debts incurred prior to the bankruptcy filing may be deemed not to be dischargeable if incurred to defraud creditors. For instance, you cannot go out and run up $10,000 of credit card debt with the idea of filing bankruptcy the next day. If you do, the $10,000 of credit card debt may not be discharged in the bankruptcy proceeding.
- ◆ Upon the filing of a bankruptcy petition there is an *automatic stay* that is entered by the court that precludes creditors (persons who claim that the debtor owes them money) from filing or pursuing any sort of civil action against the debtor. That automatic stay continues until the court lifts the stay or until there is a discharge granted to the debtor.

◆ After filing for bankruptcy, there will be a *creditor's hearing* at which time the creditors may appear and examine the debtor as to the location and extent of assets and the validity of any other debts that are claimed.

◆ Those persons who make a claim against the debtor are required to file a *proof of claim*. Those claims will then be given certain *priority*. The claims that have the highest priority are the ones that are most likely to be paid in full. Other claims that have lower priority may only be partially paid or may not be paid at all.

◆ An individual debtor is entitled to certain *exemptions* either under the bankruptcy code or pursuant to applicable state law. These exemptions allow the debtor to keep certain things. Those things may consist of items such as a motor vehicle, certain household goods, books and papers, and other things that may assist in the production of income. Exactly what property and how much money may be exempt from your creditors if you file bankruptcy, to some extent, is governed by state law. Some states are very generous to the debtor in that regard.

For instance, Florida is a state that is quite generous to debtors. Because of this, many individuals who are involved in high-risk businesses, such as real estate development, buy very expensive homes in Florida so that if their business goes under they can file for bankruptcy in Florida to hold on to that expensive home and keep it away from their creditors.

◆ The objective in most instances of a bankruptcy filing is either to gain some breathing room from the attempts by creditors to collect against the debtor or ultimately to receive a *discharge*. There are some debts, however, that are not dischargeable. Certain debts such as taxes, alimony and child support, certain student loans, and several other categories of debts may not be dischargeable.

◆ Once a discharge has been entered, the debtor is relieved of all personal liability for those discharged debts. A discharge automatically voids any judgment against the debtor for personal liability on a debt and acts as a permanent injunction prohibiting creditors from acting to recover the discharged debt from that debtor personally. The debtor may, however, *reaffirm* the debt if he or she wishes. That reaffirmation must meet specific requirements in order to be valid. To reaffirm a debt means simply that you make a new promise to pay that debt.

◆ Most contracts entered into by the debtor may be *disavowed* by the debtor. This may apply to contracts of purchase, sales, leases, etc. To disavow a contract simply means that you are stating in writing that you do not intend to honor it. Under the bankruptcy code you have that right.

Chapter 7

A Chapter 7 proceeding is one filed by an individual, partnership, or corporation wherein they have to disclose all of their debts to the court and then disclose what assets they have (if any) to satisfy those liabilities. If they have no assets to satisfy the debts, individuals will eventually be granted a discharge and their debts will be wiped out. If they do have assets to satisfy the debts, then the court may order a distribution of those assets in order to satisfy the debts before granting a discharge. A discharge under Chapter 7 may only be granted to an individual person— a partnership or corporation cannot receive a discharge. What they do get is relief from collection efforts of their creditors.

Chapter 7 filings are the most common for individuals. It is advisable for an individual filing bankruptcy to hire an experienced bankruptcy lawyer. Bankruptcy lawyers typically charge a flat fee for the handling of a Chapter 7 bankruptcy and in return for that fee they prepare all of the documents necessary for presentation to the Court, appear with you at the creditors hearing wherein you may be questioned by your creditors, and if there are any objections made to the dischargability of your debts the lawyer will represent you in regard to any proceedings relating to those issues.

In filing any bankruptcy petition it is critical that you remember that a full disclosure must be made of all debts and all assets. If you fail to do that, there could be some penalty imposed upon you by the bankruptcy court. It is also important to keep in mind that the purpose of a bankruptcy proceeding is not simply to allow you to gain some breathing room from your creditors. It is an improper motive for filing the bankruptcy action if your sole intent is to stay or forestall any collection efforts by your creditors against you with the hope that they will go away so that you can then dismiss the bankruptcy proceeding.

If it is determined that you have no assets to satisfy the debts that may be owed to your creditors, your case will be designated as a *no assets* case. The case will be concluded very quickly because your creditors will be advised that they should not file any proof of claim against you. If, however, there are assets that you have to satisfy your debts, the creditors will be advised to file their proof of claim. The creditors will then be categorized as to their priority. Creditors that are secured by a mortgage or deed of trust against a piece of real estate will have priority over creditors that are unsecured. Secured creditors may be allowed to hold onto their security and as such, their particular debt will not be discharged because there is a piece of property or other valuable item that can be used to satisfy their specific debt. Once it has been determined what the extent of your assets are that may be used to satisfy any unsecured creditors, then those assets will be divided among those various unsecured creditors based upon certain priorities established by the bankruptcy code.

As part of this bankruptcy proceeding, the debtor will eventually receive a discharge of either all of his or her debts if it is a *no assets* case, or of those debts that cannot be satisfied if there are assets to be distributed.

Before contacting a bankruptcy lawyer, make a good faith effort to deal with your creditors to see if there is some way that they can institute a payment plan. If that can be accomplished, it is more desirable than filing bankruptcy. The filing of bankruptcy is an extreme measure and should only be done if in fact your financial situation is desperate. It has harmful consequences as far as your future ability to get credit, it may have consequences as far as your employment, and does also involve a certain personal stigma.

> **NOTE: The rules, procedure, and substantive law that govern bankruptcy proceedings are unique. They are unlike many other rules that apply in civil cases. It is critical that you have an experienced bankruptcy practitioner representing you if, in fact, you are contemplating filing bankruptcy.**

Chapter 11

A second form of bankruptcy is known as a Chapter 11 filing. A Chapter 11 filing is generally referred to as a *business reorganization* and may be filed either by an individual or by a corporation. The general purpose of a Chapter 11 filing is to allow the business or individual some breathing room from the onslaught of its creditors so that the business or individual can get back on its feet and then hopefully repay the creditors in whole or in part. This type of bankruptcy involves a bankruptcy trustee who is a court official in charge of supervising the progress of the bankruptcy case.

In some Chapter 11 proceedings all of the assets of the debtor may be transferred to the trustee. This means that the debtor cannot convey any assets without approval of that trustee. The trustee may actually take over running the business of the debtor. In other cases the debtor may remain in possession of all assets. The objective of a Chapter 11 filing is to submit to the court a plan of reorganization or rehabilitation setting forth a method by which the debts and obligations of the debtor may be paid off to allow the business to continue. If that plan is not accepted by the court, then the bankruptcy filing will be dismissed. If the plan is accepted by the court, then the debtor is expected to comply with that plan over the period of time allowed. If the plan is complied with by the debtor, then the debtor will eventually come out of bankruptcy and lose the protection of the bankruptcy court.

Upon confirmation of the plan, the plan's provisions are binding on all creditors and on the debtor. Once the plan has been confirmed by the court, the debtor is discharged from all pre-confirmation debts as well as certain other types of debts.

The debtor is required to implement the plan and to comply with all court orders. The court, of course, has the authority to enforce its orders.

Some Chapter 11 cases may progress as *liquidation proceedings*. In these cases, the debtor may maintain possession of all of its assets for the purpose of gathering them together and then liquidating or selling them. This is sometimes allowed if it appears that the debtor can get more money for these assets than could the trustee in bankruptcy.

Chapter 13

A third form of bankruptcy is a Chapter 13 filing, known as a *wage earner's plan*. This type of bankruptcy can only be filed by people who receive regular wages as their form of compensation. For instance, a person who works at the phone company and receives a pay check every two weeks could file a wage earner's plan. A medical doctor, however, who works for him- or herself and receives compensation simply in the form of profits from his or her business could not file a wage earner's plan. There are also limitations on the amount of debt a person may have to file under this chapter. Under Chapter 13, a discharge is granted to the debtor once he or she has made all payments under the plan, unless it has been waived.

2005 Amendments to the Bankruptcy Code

In 2005 a number of amendments were made to the Bankruptcy Code, most of which were intended to expand the rights of creditors. Some of the more notable amendments are:

◆ A limitation of the ability of consumers with adequate income to immediately discharge unsecured debt (e.g., credit card debt) in Chapter 7 bankruptcies. This is accomplished by the needs-based test which determines whether an individual should be permitted to discharge unsecured debts under Chapter 7 or be required to pay a certain amount of these debts under a Chapter 13 five-year payment plan.

◆ New Truth-in-Lending Act disclosures banks must make to consumers regarding credit card introductory rates, Internet solicitations, and late payments penalties, among other things.

Chapter Twenty-One

Employment

The employment relationship between employer and employee is a contractual relationship. That is, if Mary offers you a job with her company and you accept that offer, then you have entered into a contract. All of the elements of a contract have been satisfied—there has been an offer made and acceptance of the offer by you, with the consideration being the wages that you will be paid in return for your services. Sometimes people enter into written contracts of employment. If there is a written contract of employment, it should be reviewed and analyzed the same as any other contract. If there is a breach of that contract by either party then there may be a resulting claim or lawsuit made for that breach of contract.

More often than not, contracts of employment are purely oral. An advertisement for the position may contain some of the terms of the contract for employment (and be written evidence of what the terms of the contract are) but the other terms of the contract, especially everything said in an interview, may be oral. That oral contract of employment is every bit as valid as a written contract of employment.

> ## It's the Law
> *More often than not, contracts of employment are purely oral.*

One caveat or restriction on that would be any limitation that may be imposed by the *statute of frauds* that may exist in that state where the employment is based. The statute of frauds is statutory law that can vary from state to state that may require that certain types of contracts be in writing to be enforceable.

Contracts that cannot be performed within one year are frequently governed by the statute of frauds. If you are offered employment for five years, and that offer and your acceptance were purely oral, that contract may not be enforceable for that five-year period because obviously a five-year employment contract cannot be performed in one year. It would therefore not be enforceable for its full term in light of the statute of frauds.

Even though a contract of employment may be in writing, there may be other evidence as to what the terms of that contract of employment are aside from any advertisements for employment and any oral agreements that may have been entered into. If the employer has an *employee manual*, the manual may set forth basic terms of employment that could be evidence of what the actual contract terms are. Likewise, such evidence could exist in any subsequent written statements relating to the employment status made by the employer or statements in writing agreed to by both the employer and the employee.

An employer is required to provide a safe work environment. If an employer fails to do that, the employer may be liable for any injuries that result. Typically, those injuries would be covered by worker's compensation insurance. (See Chapter 22.)

Discrimination

Although the foundation stone of the employment relationship is the contract, oral or written, the employment relationship is also governed by federal, state, and local statutes and ordinances. At the federal level, there are several statutes that prohibit discrimination by employers. Similar statutes may exist at the state level and also at the local level. Discrimination based upon race, sex, religion, national origin, sexual preference, and marital status may all be addressed in these different statutes and ordinances.

Federal Laws

At the federal level there are several different statutes dealing with employment discrimination. *Title VII* of the *Civil Rights Act of 1964* contained in 42 USC Sec. 2000(e) prohibits discrimination in employment, including hiring, firing, compensation, terms, conditions, or privileges of employment, on the basis of race, color, religion, sex, or national origin. This federal statute, like many federal statutes, only applies to employers that have a certain number of employees. The logic behind this requirement goes to some of the constitutional issues discussed in Chapter 1 regarding the limited authority of the federal government.

The federal government, being a government of limited authority or jurisdiction, cannot simply pass laws that govern every aspect of our lives without there being some constitutional basis for that law. The federal government is able to invoke that constitutional basis in regard to much of its legislation because of the impact that certain things may have upon *interstate commerce*. A small employer with only one employee probably has no real impact on interstate commerce. However, an employer with fifteen employees probably does have some impact, although it may be remote, on interstate commerce and therefore such employers may be governed by this federal statute.

Other federal laws concerning discrimination include the following. *Section 1981* of the *Civil Rights Act of 1866* found in 42 USC Sec. 1981 prohibits race discrimination in employment. *Section 1983* of the *Civil Rights Act of 1871* found in 42 USC Sec. 1983 prohibits discrimination on the basis of race under color of state law. What that means is that there must be a state agency or employee involved in the discriminatory act. The *Age Discrimination in Employment Act* found in 29 USC Sec. 621 covers employers with twenty or more employees and sets up a protected age group between ages forty and seventy with certain exceptions. The *Equal Pay Act* found in 29 USC Sec. 206(d) deals with discrimination in wages on the basis of sex.

Claims under *Title VII* can be brought on a theory of disparate treatment or disparate impact. *Disparate treatment* generally involves some intentional discrimination, or it can be founded upon the fact that similarly situated persons of different races receive different treatment without an adequate nonracial explanation. A *disparate impact* claim does not look at the specific treatment of individuals, rather it looks at the impact that a particular employment practice has. That is, the employment practice at issue may be neutral on its face, but the result that it has upon a particular group may be more harsh than it is on other groups. That may be a basis for a discrimination claim.

Another federal statute that may have an impact on employment is the *Americans with Disabilities Act* found at 42 USC Sec. 1210. It prohibits employers from discriminating against qualified individuals with a disability in respect to all aspects of employment, including job application procedures, hiring, advancement, or discharge. The general intent of this statute is to require employers and others to make some reasonable accommodations for disabled persons to assure that they are treated equally with other qualified individuals.

In 1993 Congress passed the *Family and Medical Leave Act*. This federal statute permits employees to take up to ninety days of paid or unpaid leave for family medical emergencies. This applies to all public sector employers and private employers with fifty or more workers. Some states have passed statutes of a similar nature.

Filing a Claim

In regard to any of these discrimination claims brought under federal law it is important to keep in mind that they may have very specific requirements that have to be met as far as how your claim is to be filed and when you can file suit. Typically the charge of discrimination has to be brought within a fairly short period of time after the discriminatory conduct by the employer. You must bring that claim to the appropriate administrative agency to investigate it. Then you must either await the conclusion at that administrative level or await the passage of a certain amount of time before you can actually file suit against the employer. All of those requirements are very specific and dictated by the statute that you are suing under.

It's the Law

You must bring a discrimination claim to the appropriate administrative agency before filing suit.

State and Local Laws

Similar types of requirements may be called for in regard to any claims brought under state statutory provisions or local ordinances. The general framework of these statutes is to require that the employee bring the claim promptly so that the employer is given notice of the charge made by the employee, thereby giving the employer the opportunity to investigate the claim. Likewise, the appropriate federal or state agency can investigate the claim. If that investigation does not resolve the matter, then the employee will eventually acquire the right to file a civil action against the employer.

At-Will Employment

In many states, in the absence of an express contract for employment, an employee is considered to be an *employee at will*. An employee at will is free to leave that employment at any time the employee wishes and likewise the employer is free to terminate the employment any time it wishes. When the employee is considered to be an employee at will, the only restriction imposed upon the employer is simply that he or she cannot terminate the employment for a discriminatory reason in violation of federal, state, or local statutes that may apply and likewise may not terminate the employment for a reason that would violate what is referred to as *public policy*.

For instance, an employee discovers that the employer is defrauding the federal government with whom it has a contract. The employee complains of that and thereafter is terminated for that reason. Even though the employment relationship in that context may have been *at will*, the employee may still have a basis for a wrongful discharge claim against the employer.

Overtime and Minimum Wage

Compensation for overtime work is governed by the *Fair Labor Standards Act* found at 29 USC Secs. 201, *et seq*. In general, *nonexempt employees* are entitled to overtime pay if they work more than forty hours in a seven-day workweek. If your workweek is Monday through Friday and you report to work at 8:30 a.m., receive thirty minutes for lunch with no job duties imposed upon you during that lunch break, and leave work at 5:00 p.m., you have worked a forty-hour week. If you worked more than that in a seven-day workweek, then you may be entitled to overtime. Many employers require employees to report to work at 9:00 a.m., allow thirty minutes or more for lunch, with the employees then leaving at 5:00 p.m. A workweek such as that is actually a 37½-hour week. No overtime would be required until you hit the forty-hour mark.

People who are just entering the work force may be offered *minimum wage* positions. As of 2009, the federal minimum wage is $7.25. That is, employers are required by law to pay that much per hour for most positions. There are some exemptions. Your state may impose a higher minimum wage amount.

Unemployment

Unemployment compensation laws are an aspect of employment law. *Unemployment compensation* is a state and federal funding system to provide compensation to people who are unemployed for a period of time.

If you are laid off from your position, you may be entitled to unemployment compensation benefits for a certain period of time. Those benefits do not go on forever. The expectation is that eventually you will find new work and therefore the benefits do have a termination date.

Your entitlement to unemployment compensation benefits may differ by state. In general, however, you are entitled to unemployment compensation benefits unless you voluntarily left your employment or unless you were dismissed from the employment due to some misconduct on your part. The misconduct typically must be fairly serious in order to defeat your claim for unemployment compensation benefits.

Severance and Layoffs

When an employer ends employment of an employee, in some instances that employee may receive severance pay. There generally is no statutory or legal right to severance pay. A *severance package* may be offered by an employer as a way of buying the employee's cooperation, and further as a way of securing or providing consideration for a release of any claims that the employee may have against the employer.

In those instances where there are mass layoffs by an employer, that employer needs to be mindful of federal, state, and local discrimination laws in terms of how the laid off employees are chosen. That is, if the laid off employees are all persons over 50 years of age, then there may be problems with the *Age Discrimination in Employment Act*. If all of the laid off employees are female, there may be problems with federal *Civil Rights* statutes.

Chapter Twenty-Two

Workers' Compensation

Workers' compensation is a form of insurance coverage that is designed to protect the working person in the event of injury. In a workers' compensation claim the parties involved are the injured worker, his or her employer, and the employer's workers' compensation insurance company. Before the passage of workers' compensation laws, a worker who was injured on the job was forced to file suit against his or her employer and potentially wait for months or even years before ever receiving any compensation for an injury.

As a result, the worker and his or her family may have had no income for an extended period of time because the worker was injured and unable to work. Further, the worker often was unable to pay for medical treatment. If the worker did eventually recover from the employer in a civil action, that award of money damages frequently came too late for the worker since by that point he or she was destitute and perhaps permanently impaired because of the lack of proper medical treatment.

As such, many states began passing workers' compensation laws that provided a type of compromise. Under these laws, the worker did not have to prove any fault on the part of the employer when injured, but simply had to prove that he or she was on the job and that the injury arose out of his or her employment. If those two things could be proven, then the worker was entitled to receive a portion of his or her wages for the period of time disabled and further was entitled to appropriate medical treatment related to that injury.

In return for that, the employer received immunity from a civil claim brought by the employee for the injury. That is, the employee could not file a civil action against the employer. The employee's exclusive remedy is the worker's compensation benefits.

Every state has its own workers' compensation law and that law can vary dramatically from state to state. The general thrust, however, of the worker's compensation system nationwide is as stated.

In addition, there are workers' compensation acts that operate at the federal level. Individuals employed by the federal government are covered by the Federal *Employees Compensation Act.* It is a workers' compensation act that is administered by the U.S. Department of Labor. There is also another federal statute known as the *Longshoremen and Harbor Worker's Act,* which technically covers longshoreman and harbor workers but includes private, nonfederal employees who are working on defense installations as well. It also covers private employees working overseas who are covered by the *Defense Base Act*—a type of workers' compensation act that incorporates the *Longshoremen and Harbor Workers Act.*

> ## It's the Law
> *In most states, an employee's exclusive remedy is workers' compensation benefits.*

Claims

Workers' compensation acts around the country are administered by a governmental agency for that jurisdiction. If an employee is injured on the job, he or she must report that injury to his or her employer within a designated period of time and file a written report of that injury. If the employee is forced to lose time from work or requires medical treatment, then he or she may file a claim with the administrative agency that administers workers' compensation claims for that jurisdiction. Once a claim is filed, the employer can either contest or accept the claim.

If the employer accepts the claim, then the employer is agreeing that the employee was injured on the job, that the injury arose out of the employment, and that the employee is entitled to medical coverage and perhaps to wage benefits for the time disabled. If the employer decides to challenge the claim, there will be a hearing before an administrative law judge or a hearing officer who will then make a decision whether the claim is compensable and whether the employee should be paid wage benefits and/or medical benefits.

There has been a good bit of litigation over the years as to exactly what constitutes being an employee. Typically a person who is an *independent contractor* will not qualify as an employee under the workers' compensation act. Likewise, the individual who is the owner of the business may not qualify as an employee unless he or she has expressly chosen to include him- or herself in that definition within the policy of insurance issued.

Benefits

Wage benefits are calculated based upon the *average weekly wage*—the wages of the employee over a period of time are totaled up and then averaged. Once that average has been calculated, the employee is typically entitled to two-thirds of that average weekly wage (up to a statutory ceiling).

The second form of benefit received under workers' compensation is medical coverage. If an employee is injured on the job, he or she is entitled to reasonable and necessary hospital and medical treatment related to that injury to hopefully get him or her back on his or her feet and able to resume his or her employment. If the employee is not able to resume his or her former employment, then he or she may be entitled to rehabilitation services that will either allow him or her to return to some other form of employment or be trained in a new line of work.

A final type of compensation that the employee may be entitled to as a result of an on-the-job injury is compensation for permanent disability. Most workers' compensation acts have created a schedule in which specific disabilities are worth a certain number of weeks of wages. For instance, a person who loses a foot may be entitled to one hundred and fifty weeks of wages over and above any other benefits that he or she may receive. A person who loses an eye on the job may be entitled to an equivalent amount of compensation. Those forms of compensation are in addition to the wage loss benefits otherwise paid and any medical expenses that have been paid.

Death Benefits

In the event that an employee is killed on the job, the family of that employee is entitled to death benefits. Those death benefits are wage benefits that will, at least in part, replace the loss of income as a result of the death of the employee.

Capping Benefits

There has been a good deal of controversy over the extent to which workers' compensation laws should provide benefits to injured employees. Many states put a *cap* on the amount of wage benefits that the employee can receive. In some jurisdictions the employee can receive no more than five hundred weeks of wage benefits, which is the equivalent of approximately ten years of benefits. This is to the advantage of the employer in that it puts a limitation on the employer's or the insurer's liability.

However, it may be a detriment to the employee if the employee is permanently disabled and cannot return to any form of work. If in fact the employee is permanently and totally disabled, then he or she may be able to extend those benefits under state law. However, proving that a worker is both permanently and totally disabled is not an easy task. As such, in many states employees are left in a situation in which they cannot return to their former employment, yet at the end of the allowable time their wage benefits are terminated.

Medical Treatment

There also is a good bit of controversy regarding the provision of medical treatment to injured workers. Typically, the medical treatment is controlled by the employer or the employer's insurance carrier. This means that the employee receives treatment from doctors who have been chosen by the insurance carrier or the employer. These doctors obviously know who is paying their bill and they know that the insurance carrier and the employer expect this employee to return to work at some point in time so that their financial exposure in paying wage benefits is limited.

Although these doctors generally provide quality medical care for the injured employee, they have a somewhat mixed loyalty. They know that the employer and the insurance company want this employee to return to work, but they also know that it is not necessarily always in the employee's interest to return to work too quickly or even to return to that form of work at all.

Complex Injuries

The law relating to workers' compensation coverage can become extremely complex when dealing with issues of occupational disease. The run-of-the-mill, on-the-job injury in which an employee falls and breaks an ankle does not involve a great deal of controversy. However, the claim of the employee who over a period of time develops, for example, carpal tunnel syndrome as a result of typing at the keyboard, is harder to classify as being a result of the employment. Different states have dealt with that issue in a variety of ways. Some states provide coverage for these types of repetitive stress injuries or exposure injuries; other states do not.

Another area of significant controversy in regard to workers' compensation claims is compensation for emotional injuries. In some states, an employee who suffers, for example, a nervous breakdown because of emotional stress on the job may be entitled to the whole range of benefits under the workers' compensation system. Other states have denied those types of benefits on the theory that the relationship between employment and emotional injury is simply too tenuous and therefore the employer should not be made to bear the burden of the expense associated with that type of injury.

Third-Party Claims

If an employee is injured on the job as a result of the fault of some third person, then that employee may have a basis for a claim (sometimes referred to as a *third-party claim*) against that other individual or company. For instance, suppose you are working on a construction job and you are employed by the general contractor. If, while performing those duties, an employee of a plumbing sub-contractor drops a pipe that strikes you on the head, you may be entitled to the benefits called for under the act. In addition to being compensated under the workers' compensation act, you may also have a basis for a claim against the plumbing sub-contractor whose employee dropped the pipe on you. In some states, on a construction job such as this, all contractors may be immune from suit by any other employee on that construction job. In other states, the employee may sue any other responsible contractor on the job.

If the injured employee in that circumstance does recover money from the third party who caused the injury, then the employer of that injured worker (or more likely the employer's insurance carrier) is entitled to recover all or part of the monies paid to the worker under the workers' compensation act. This is a principle known as *subrogation*. Subrogation literally means that one party is subrogated or steps into the shoes of another party and acquires their rights.

Under most workers' compensation acts, once the employee makes a claim for and receives benefits, then to the extent that the employee has any right of recovery against a third party, the employer or its insurance carrier acquires that right of recovery to the extent of wage and income benefits it paid to the employee. The purpose of allowing subrogation in this instance is to hold down the cost of workers' compensation insurance coverage and further to prevent the employee from receiving a double recovery on the wages and medical benefits received.

If the employee receives compensation under the workers' compensation act and is further compensated for the same injuries as a result of the third-party civil claim, that constitutes a *double recovery* to the employee. After paying back amounts paid to him for wage and medical benefits under the workers' compensation act, the employee is entitled to keep any excess damages awarded by a jury or received in settlement.

Second Injury Fund
and Uninsured Employer Fund

Workers' compensation claims can be complicated when an individual has suffered an injury while employed with one company and then goes to work for another company and later reinjures him- or herself. Which employer is going to be responsible for that compensation?

Some states have set up what is referred to as a *second injury fund*. In these states, that second injury will be partially paid out of that second injury fund and then also partially paid by the second company. That second injury fund is a fund of money that is created by contributions from all of the different insurance companies that underwrite workers' compensation insurance coverage in that jurisdiction.

A similar type of fund that may exist is the *uninsured employer's fund*. An employer who has not taken out workers' compensation coverage and who therefore cannot pay the benefits called for under the workers' compensation act may still be covered in the sense that the employee may make a claim against the uninsured employer's fund. To the extent that any payments are made out of that fund, the fund administrator or the attorney general of that state will typically make a claim against the uninsured employer in order to recover such payments.

Chapter Twenty-Three

Insurance

An insurance policy is a contract. The parties to the contract are the insurance company and the insured. In addition, there may be a *beneficiary* or what may be referred to as a *third-party beneficiary* of an insurance contract. In a life insurance policy, the beneficiary is the person who receives the death benefits upon the death of a person who was insured. In an automobile insurance policy, the third-party beneficiary under a liability policy is the individual who was injured and who receives compensation from that liability insurance policy. The beneficiary or third-party beneficiary is not a named party to the insurance contract, but is generally the person who is intended to benefit from the insurance policy. As such, that beneficiary may have certain rights under the policy.

There are a variety of different types of insurance policies that can be written. The most common types of policies are liability, life insurance, and health insurance policies.

Automobile Insurance

The type of insurance coverage that you are probably most familiar with is *automobile insurance* coverage. An automobile policy may include several different forms of coverage. Within one policy there may be *liability coverage*, there may be *medical expense coverage*, there may be *collision coverage*, and there may be *uninsured motorist* and *underinsured motorist coverage*. Each of those types of coverage is dramatically different and each of them has a different objective.

Liability coverage is designed to protect you, the insured, in the event you are involved in a collision in which some other person is injured as a result of your alleged negligence. If a person is injured and they contend that you are negligent, then they may assert a liability claim against you for their medical expenses, lost wages, pain and suffering, resulting disabilities, disfigurement, etc.

Your liability insurance policy would cover you in that instance by providing you with an attorney to defend you in that claim and by *indemnifying* (reimbursing) you for any judgment rendered against you in that case up to your policy limits. If your policy limits are $50,000, but the judgment entered against you is for $500,000, then your insurance company is only obliged to pay $50,000. The remaining $450,000 may come out of your pocket.

Also within an automobile insurance policy there may be *comprehensive coverage.* Comprehensive coverage is a type of *first party coverage* wherein you may make a claim against your own policy as a result of damage to your vehicle. If your vehicle was damaged in a collision and you do not wish to or cannot assert a claim against the other party (or if you were at fault), then you may make a claim against your own policy under your collision coverage. Your insurance company will then pay you for the repair cost of your vehicle. In the event your vehicle is *totaled,* it will pay you the *fair market value* for that vehicle. If someone other than you was at fault, your insurance company may then have a right of recovery against that other driver.

Most forms of collision coverage do carry a *deductible.* This means that you would only be compensated by your insurance carrier for the amount of money that exceeded your deductible amount.

Auto insurance coverage also offers what is referred to as *medical expense coverage* or *personal injury protection coverage.* This is a type of *first party coverage* wherein you may make a claim against your own insurance company for medical expenses incurred as a result of a collision. If you are injured in an automobile collision while in your car, you can make a claim against your policy for payment of your medical expenses to the extent that they were reasonable and necessary as a result of this collision. If you are a passenger in someone else's vehicle, then, assuming there is medical payments coverage for the vehicle you are riding in, you can make a claim for medical payments under that policy. You may be able to make a claim for medical payments under your own policy, too.

Another form of coverage under a typical automobile insurance policy is *uninsured motorist* and *underinsured motorist coverage*. This is a very important form of coverage because it protects you in the event that you are involved in a collision that is the fault of an uninsured or underinsured motorist.

Example: *Suppose you are hit from the rear by a vehicle that is uninsured and you are injured. You could sue the driver of that striking vehicle, but he or she may have no assets to pay any judgment that you may obtain against him or her. In that instance, your own uninsured motorist coverage would apply. In such an event your insurance company could essentially step in and defend that uninsured motorist, or at least take a position that is contrary to you, by challenging your claims for uninsured motorist benefits.*

The same basic principle would apply if that striking vehicle was underinsured.

Example: *Suppose the vehicle that struck you from behind has $25,000 in coverage but your medical expenses as a result of the collision are $50,000. The striking motorist would then be underinsured. If you got a judgment for your medical expenses, he or she may not be able to pay it. His or her insurance policy would pay the first $25,000, but anything beyond that would be covered by your policy to the extent that you had underinsured motorist coverage.*

Uninsured motorist coverage is a very broad form of coverage. Even if you are a bicyclist or a pedestrian struck by an uninsured

It's the Law

If you are struck by a hit-and-run motorist, you may make a claim under your own uninsured motorist coverage.

motorist (or by a hit-and-run motorist), you may make a claim for and recover under your own uninsured motorist coverage.

Life Insurance

Another form of insurance is *life insurance* coverage. A life insurance policy is simply a contract between you—the insured—and the insurance company wherein the insurance company agrees to pay a certain amount of benefits upon your death. Assuming that there have been no misrepresentations made by you in applying for this type of insurance coverage, then your survivors would simply make a claim to that insurance company upon your passing and the designated beneficiary will then receive the benefits due.

There are different types of life insurance coverage. The most common form of life insurance coverage these days is *term life insurance*. Term life insurance policies have no value other than the face amount of the policy, and even then have no value unless the person who is insured passes away during the coverage period.

Another type of life insurance coverage is that of *whole life coverage*. This is actually a type of investment in which the value of the policy may increase over a period of time as you pay premiums. You may also be allowed to take loans against the policy and perhaps even redeem the policy for a fixed amount of money. The theory behind whole life is that you not only are insuring your life, but you are also making an investment that is increasing in value over a period of time that you may utilize by taking a loan against it or cashing it in.

In most life insurance policies, the application for insurance is included as part of the policy. The reason for that is that payments under life insurance policies are generally rather substantial. If there are any misrepresentations made in the application, that may be a basis for voiding the insurance policy. Frequently those misrepresentations are not discovered until after the person has passed away and an autopsy has been performed.

Health Insurance

Another type of insurance coverage is *health insurance*. Health insurance contracts are frequently group insurance contracts wherein you, as a member of a group, pay a premium to the insurance company in return for the insurance company agreeing to cover medical and hospital expenses up to certain limits. The general limitation of the scope of coverage under these policies is that the treatment that you receive must be reasonable and necessary and the cost of the treatment must be consistent with the usual and customary charges for other practitioners in the area.

For instance, if you decide to have plastic surgery that is purely elective, this type of treatment may not be covered unless you have a special endorsement or provision within your policy that provides coverage since the treatment is not necessary. Likewise, if you choose to go to the most expensive orthopedic surgeon in the area because you think he or she is the best, all of the charges rendered by that surgeon may not be covered under your policy. The policy is governed by what is *usual and customary* for those types of services and not necessarily by what the best practitioner in that area may charge.

Homeowners Insurance

Another type of insurance coverage is *homeowners insurance* coverage. A homeowners policy typically includes a fire endorsement, which would cover you in the event that your house, including contents, burns down. It is important that you make sure that the stated value is consistent with the replacement cost or the fair market value of the house when reviewing this type of coverage. For instance, if you are in a geographical area where property values are increasing dramatically, then it is important that you likewise increase the covered amount under this provision of your homeowners policy to make sure that there is enough money paid to you in the event that your house does burn down. Likewise, within this type of policy there may be coverage for water damage, theft, and also for liability claims.

Liability may arise in a homeowner's context when a guest is on your premises and is injured as a result of some defect on the premises. For instance, suppose there is a large hole in your backyard that is covered by overgrown grass and your guest falls into that hole and breaks an ankle. If you knew of the hole and did not disclose it, then the guest may have a basis for a liability claim against you alleging that there is negligence on your part. If a judge or jury were to agree with that, then the liability insurance policy would have to indemnify you up to your policy limits. Under this type of liability policy, the liability insurance carrier would also provide an attorney to defend you.

Under a homeowners policy, if there are specific valuable items of personal property that you wish to have covered, they normally have to be covered under a *scheduled loss section* of the policy where the specific items are identified. There may even be a requirement that an appraisal or pictures of the objects be provided as part of the insurance policy.

Malpractice Insurance

If you are a medical doctor, you most likely have a *malpractice insurance* policy covering you. That malpractice policy is a form of liability coverage that would apply in an instance where a patient sues you for malpractice. In that event, the malpractice insurance company would step in, conduct an investigation, and determine if the claim should be adjusted or negotiated. Some medical malpractice policies require the consent of the doctor before any settlement offers can be made. In the event the insurance company does not settle your patient's claim, the patient may file suit against you. The insurance company would appoint an attorney to represent you and then would indemnify you as to any judgment up to the amount of your policy limits.

Insurance Agents

Most insurance is sold through *insurance agents*. Insurance agents are frequently referred to as *dual agents*. That is, they are both an agent of the company that underwrites the insurance policy and also the person who applies for the insurance policy. To say that they are a dual agent means that they have certain duties to each party—certain duties to the underwriter and also certain duties to the insured.

Chapter Twenty-Four
Internet Law

Any discussion of Internet law (or "cyber law") should start with the warning that the combination of the words "Internet" and "law" in the same phrase is a bit of a contradiction in terms. Despite the dominating existence of the Internet, our sluggish legislative system remains far behind even the not-so-recent advances in technology. While our legislatures are slowly catching up, many areas of Internet law remain largely uncharted territory. With that said, it is especially important that any legal questions you may have involving the Internet should be directed to a licensed attorney. This section does, however, attempt to address the major Internet law issues that may impact the average reader.

Jurisdictional Issues

First, and perhaps most importantly, the Internet has drastically expanded the reach of courts and the jurisdictions in which individuals and companies may be sued. With the Internet, the once costly phone call to the distant merchant in Oregon now can occur by email, instant messaging, or online for free. As technology continues to shrink the size of our planet through easy access to distant locations, the threat that you may be subject to a lawsuit in a state or country you have never actually visited has increased dramatically. For example, Virginia is known as a *single act* state, which means even a single act directed at a company or resident in Virginia *may* subject a person outside of Virginia to being sued in a Virginia court. Virginia courts have held that sending a single email or accessing a publicly available website may qualify as the single necessary act.

Defamation

With the increasing popularity of Internet blogs, personal Web sites, chat rooms, and social networking sites, a new and easier form of defamation has emerged. The term *defamation* refers to a false statement made about someone or some organization that is damaging to their reputation. (See pp.136–137.) While defamation is largely the same whether committed online or by more traditional means, the significance of Internet defamation is the danger posed by widespread public access to the Internet and the ability for a seemingly innocent rant to spread quickly through Internet websites, emails, and online postings. Importantly, under the *Communications Decency Act* (codified at 47 U.S.C. § 230), website owners generally cannot be held liable for defamatory or otherwise harmful content posted on their site by third parties.

Contracts

The reader may have noticed that on a daily basis they are asked by websites and online merchants to "accept the terms and conditions" of online transactions. Typically this involves clicking on a small icon titled "accept" or "yes." While you may laugh as you scroll past the never-ending list of online terms and conditions, if you think you will not be bound by those terms because you do not read them or sign anything, you may be sadly mistaken. These types of online contracts are increasingly upheld by courts under the view that clicking on the icon titled "accept" or "yes" indicates acceptance of the terms and is the equivalent of an electronic signature. Moreover, many states have adopted the *Uniform Electronic Transactions Act*, which serves to uphold electronic documents that are accepted by some affirmative act indicating acceptance.

In addition, ignoring the lengthy terms and conditions can have important consequences. For example, often these terms and conditions will designate a particular state and forum where a lawsuit may be filed, known as a forum-selection clause (typically the state and forum will be the one most convenient for the person/entity that is asking you to accept the terms). In addition, these terms may also include: (1) a limitation on the amount you can sue for, typically limited to the purchase price or transaction amount, or in some cases a waiver of any liability; (2) a waiver of your right to a jury trial; (3) an arbitration clause in which you are bound to arbitrate any dispute as opposed to filing suit; and (4) a clause designating a particular state's law as governing any dispute.

Identify Theft

Identity theft occurs when a criminal uses personal information to steal someone's identity. Identity theft can occur in a variety of different ways, including misuse of a Social Security number, counterfeit credit cards in your name, and mail fraud. Until relatively recently, identity theft fell under the umbrella of the charges of theft, larceny, or conversion. Identify theft, however, is one area of the law where legislatures are rapidly catching up with the technology. The Internet has made identity theft an increasing problem as wireless Internet connections can provide sophisticated "hackers" with access to your computer and phone, both of which may contain personal and financial information. States and the federal government are making huge strides in combating the problem by enacting and amending various statutes, including:

Fair Credit Reporting Act

The *Fair Credit Reporting Act* establishes procedures for correcting mistakes on your credit record and requires that your record only be provided for legitimate business needs.

Fair Credit Billing Act

The *Fair Credit Billing Act* establishes procedures for resolving billing errors on your credit card accounts. It also limits a consumer's liability for fraudulent credit card charges.

Fair Debt Collection Practices Act

The *Fair Debt Collection Practices Act* prohibits debt collectors from using unfair or deceptive practices to collect overdue bills that your creditor has forwarded for collection.

Electronic Fund Transfer Act

The *Electronic Fund Transfer Act* provides consumer protection for all transactions using a debit card or electronic means to debit or credit an account. It also limits a consumer's liability for unauthorized electronic fund transfers.

Identity Theft and Assumption Deterrence Act

Enacted by Congress in October 1998 (and codified, in part, at 18 U.S.C. §1028), the *Identify Theft and Assumption Deterrence Act* makes identity theft a federal crime.

Under federal criminal law, identity theft takes place when someone "knowingly transfers, possesses, or uses, without lawful authority, a means of identification of another person with the intent to commit, or to aid or abet, or in connection with, any unlawful activity that constitutes a violation of federal law, or that constitutes a felony under any applicable state or local law." Under this definition, a name, Social Security number, or credit card are all considered a "means of identification."

Violations of the ITADA are investigated by federal law enforcement agencies, including the U.S. Secret Service, the FBI, the U.S. Postal Inspection Service, and the Social Security Administration's Office of the Inspector General. Federal identity theft cases are prosecuted by the U.S. Department of Justice.

In 2004, Congress passed the *Identity Theft Penalty Enhancement Act*. This act established a mandatory two-year minimum sentence to be served in addition to the sentence that a person may have been already sentenced to for aggravated identity theft.

Many states have also enacted statutes which not only require credit agencies to block inaccurate information resulting from identity theft, but specifically create a separate crime for identity theft and require government agencies to assist the victim with repairing his/her credit report. Many states also permit individuals to place a credit freeze or fraud alert on their credit report while the identity theft is being resolved.

Spam

In 2003, Congress passed the *Controlling the Assault of Non-Solicited Pornography and Marketing Act*, otherwise known as the CAN-SPAM Act of 2003. The CAN-SPAM Act prohibits the distribution of certain unsolicited electronic mail, or "spam." The Act imposes both monetary penalties and incarceration upon violators but does not create a private cause of action on the part of the recipient of spam. Instead, the Act is enforced by a combination of Federal Trade Commission proceedings, criminal prosecution, state attorney general actions, and private lawsuits brought by Internet service providers. Penalties can be severe, and if the violations of the Act are committed willingly and knowingly, or if the violation included harvesting email addresses or the automatic creation of electronic mail addresses, the court may treble the damages awarded.

The Act makes it a crime to send unsolicited commercial electronic mail containing fraudulent header information and prohibits certain methods of generating electronic mail address lists. The Act further prohibits the transmission of commercial electronic mail to recipients who have "opted out" of receiving such communications from the sender. It also creates a regulatory scheme by which certain identifying information is required in all commercial electronic mail and directs the Federal Trade Commission (FTC) to develop a plan for implementing a national Do-Not-Email registry.

It is important to note that many states have also enacted their own version of anti-spam acts. While the federal Act preempts most of these state statutes, the federal Act does not preempt state laws that are not specific to spam, including state trespass, contract, or tort law. Similarly, the federal Act does not preempt states laws that relate to acts of fraud or computer crimes. With regard to computer crimes, most states have also enacted computer crime laws that carry severe criminal penalties. Though a full summary of the various computer crime laws is beyond the scope of this book, generally speaking, unauthorized access to a computer or computer network is a criminal act. Indeed, unauthorized access to a computer that is used in interstate or foreign commerce or communication is a federal crime under the *Computer Fraud and Abuse Act* (CFAA), codified at 18 U.S.C. § 1030. If this same conduct is performed for the transmission of unsolicited bulk electronic mail, penalties can be more severe, with courts increasingly categorizing this type of conduct as not only a violation of anti-spam statutes but also a form of trespass to property.

Internet Harassment/Stalking

The relatively recent popularity of social networking sites has created a whole new breed of criminal, specifically with regard to stalking, harassment, and child endangerment. Though states are increasingly enacting laws to protect individuals (and particularly children) from these types of dangers, it is important to discuss this with an attorney or the local authorities if you feel you or your child may be a victim of improper Internet conduct. While the federal government has enacted an Anti-Cyber-Stalking law, the *Violence Against Women Act* (which also protects against cyber-stalking), and the *Children's Internet Protection Act* (CIPA) (which protects children from access to offensive content over the Internet on certain school and library computers), there remains a noticeable lack of federal legislation in this area and the law is still evolving. Absent the passage of new federal laws directed at Internet harassment or stalking, the government has had to rely on older statutes such as the CFAA in order to prosecute individuals for these actions. Federal prosecutors have brought these charges on the theory that the defendant violated a website's terms of use, and therefore violated the conditions under which they were given authorized access to the site, when they used the site to harass or intimidate another person. The substantive legislative acts involving cyber-stalking have occurred at the state level. While federal and state laws on cyber-stalking typically require some form of actual or implied threat for there to be criminal conduct, many foreign countries have recently criminalized broader forms of cyber-stalking, including more general forms of online abuse, malicious communication, harassment, and cyber-bullying. It should be noted that the states are increasingly recognizing the danger of Internet harassment and cyber-bullying. As such, the law on this issue is bound to change in the near future to address the dangers of this sort of conduct.

With that said, it is important to note that the information posted on social networking sites is public information that frequently can be viewed by anyone with Internet access. The reader should pay particular attention to embarrassing or highly personal information that may be posted for friends' enjoyment, though can also be viewed by strangers, criminals, and employers.

Copyright and Trademark Infringement

One increasingly litigated area of Internet law involves copyright and trademark infringement. Websites are increasingly listed/ranked by search engines based on coding known as "meta tags." Sophisticated businesses use competitors' logos and trademarks within the metatags in order to increase their search engine ranking and thereby increase their Internet exposure. Used properly, this form of keyword advertising dramatically increases the number of visitors to, and sales by, a particular website. At the same time, this practice has lead to litigation over copyright and trademark laws.

According to the *Lanham Trademark Act*, a trademark is "any word, name, symbol, or device, or any combination thereof... used by a person, or...[intended for use in commerce]...to identify and distinguish his or her goods...from those manufactured or sold by others and to indicate the source of the goods, even if that source is unknown." A trademark serves as a form of source indicator for consumers, allowing them to associate the product with its manufacturer. For example, the Coca-Cola name and logo carry a certain reputation of quality and reliability that a consumer can associate with products with that name or logo.

The Lanham Trademark Act provides federal protection for both registered and unregistered trademarks, though additional benefits may apply to those that are registered, with the greatest protection being afforded to highly distinctive marks. The Lanham Act prohibits both infringement and dilution, permitting trademark owners to obtain injunctions, and in some cases monetary damages, for the improper use of their marks. Copying and pasting a trademark or logo onto a website or for use in the metatags can carry severe consequences and should only be done after conferring with a licensed attorney.

Chapter Twenty-Five
Privacy Law

Until fairly recent times, the law of privacy was limited to a narrow set of privacy rights found in constitutional law and the common law of torts. However, as individuals, corporations, and governments have come to rely increasingly on technology to communicate, complete transactions, and store information, more and more sensitive information is at risk to hackers and data thieves. Thus, vast opportunities have been created for the unscrupulous to surreptitiously collect sensitive information and to bombard people with unwanted advertisements and solicitations. This has led the states and the federal government to enact a wide swath of privacy laws to ensure that sensitive information is adequately protected and personal privacy is not lost with the advent of the information age. This chapter will briefly discuss the traditional privacy protections provided under the Constitution and common law, followed by a summary of some of the more prominent privacy statutes enacted in recent years.

The Federal Constitution

The text of the federal constitution does not specifically mention a "right to privacy." However, several of the amendments in the Bill of Rights have been interpreted as providing protection against certain governmental invasions of privacy. Additionally, some state constitutions provide broad privacy protections against actions by both government and private actors.

Most of the Supreme Court's discussion of the right to privacy has focused on the Fourth Amendment's protections from warrantless or unreasonable searches and seizures by the government. However, the Fourth Amendment does not provide the

It's the Law

Even though a "right to privacy" is not specifically mentioned in the federal constitution's Bill of Rights, courts have interpreted several constitutional amendments as providing protection against certain governmental invasions of privacy.

only constitutional privacy rights. In fact, courts have found that the First, Third, Fifth, Ninth, Tenth, and Fourteenth Amendments also provide certain privacy rights. For example, the right to freedom of association embodied in the First Amendment makes it unconstitutional for the government to require private associations to disclose their membership lists. Additionally, the Supreme Court has found a constitutional right to "marital privacy" inherent in the privacy rights afforded by the Fifth and Ninth Amendments, among others.

State Constitutions

Many states have passed constitutional amendments that afford a right to privacy that is similar, and in some cases even broader, than the rights afforded by the federal constitution. For example, the California constitution states that among its citizens' "inalienable rights" is the right to pursue and obtain privacy. Additionally, the California Supreme Court has interpreted this provision as applying to private as well as government actors. The Hawaiian constitution also specifically mentions a right to privacy, and this was the basis for a Hawaiian Supreme Court decision approving of same-sex marriage, although the state constitution was later amended to outlaw gay marriage.

Common Law Privacy Rights

The law of torts has long recognized a cause of action to protect against unreasonable interferences with a person's solitude. The tort of invasion of privacy can take one of four forms:

1. *Appropriation of an Individual's Picture or Name.* This particular brand of invasion of privacy requires the plaintiff to prove that the defendant made unauthorized use of the plaintiff's picture or name for the defendant's commercial advantage.

2. *Intrusion on an Individual's Affairs or Seclusion.* This cause of action requires the plaintiff to prove the defendant pried or intruded on the plaintiff's private affairs in a manner that would be objectionable to a reasonable person.

3. *False Light.* This tort requires the plaintiff to prove public disclosure of facts that place the plaintiff in a false light that would be objectionable to a reasonable person under the circumstances. Where the facts at issue are a matter of public interest, the plaintiff must also be able to prove that the defendant acted with malice.

4. *Public Disclosure of Private Facts.* This form of invasion of privacy requires publication or public disclosure by the defendant of private information about the plaintiff such that a reasonable person would object to having it made public. The defendant may be liable under this theory even if the facts are true, although if it is a matter of public interest the plaintiff must additionally prove that the defendant acted with malice.

Statutory Privacy Rights

A number of state and federal statutes also afford individuals certain privacy rights. The state laws are generally enforced by state attorneys general, while the federal laws are typically enforced by one or more federal agencies, such as the Federal Trade Commission (FTC), Federal Communications Commission (FCC), or Securities and Exchange Commission (SEC). When a state attorney general or federal agency opens an investigation into a violation of these privacy laws, the investigation often ends with the target of the investigation entering into what is called a "consent decree." Generally, the consent decree will require the target of the investigation to discontinue its prior

> ### It's the Law
> *Some state constitutions specifically recognize a broader right to privacy than the federal constitution. Additionally, the constitutions of some states (e.g., California) protect privacy rights against actions by both government and private actors.*

illegal activities, to take certain measures to ensure that the violations will not be repeated, and often includes a monetary fine. State attorneys general and the FTC also have authority to investigate any unfair or deceptive trade practices that companies engage in during their dealings with consumers. For example, if a company's privacy policy states that it takes certain steps to protect the personal information it collects from consumers, when in fact it takes no such precautions, it may be investigated by the FTC for committing a deceptive trade practice.

As always, if federal law does not preempt state regulation, states are permitted to pass privacy laws that cover the same subject matter as federal law. In these instances, states can pass laws that provide more privacy protections than federal law, but they are never permitted to pass laws that provide fewer rights than federal law. In this sense, federal law acts as a floor, rather than a ceiling, for privacy protections. Here is a summary of some of the more prominent federal laws that protect privacy and personal information:

Children's Online Privacy Protection Act (COPPA)

COPPA applies to commercial websites and online services directed to children under the age of 13 or those that have actual knowledge they are collecting personal information from children under 13. Among other things, covered entities must: (1) obtain verifiable parental consent before they collect personal information from children; (2) give parents a choice as to whether their child's personal information can be disclosed to third parties; and (3) give parents the opportunity to delete the child's personal information.

Controlling the Assault of Non-Solicited Pornography and Marketing Act (CAN-SPAM)

CAN-SPAM applies to email directed to or originating from the U.S. whose primary purpose is advertising or promoting a commercial product or service, including content on a website. The law bans false or misleading header information (*i.e.*, the "from," "to," and routing information, including the originating domain name and email address). It also: (1) prohibits deceptive subject lines; (2) requires that email give recipients a method to opt-out of receiving any future emails; and (3) requires that commercial email be identified as an advertisement and include the sender's valid physical postal address.

Wiretap Act

The *Wiretap Act* prohibits the government and individuals from intentionally intercepting, using, or disclosing wire, oral, or electronic communications. However, this general rule is subject to some exceptions. For example, when authorized by the Justice Department and signed by a United States District Court or Court of Appeals judge, a wiretap order permits law enforcement to intercept communications for up to thirty days. Also, interception, use, or disclosure of a communication is permissible when one of the parties to the communication has given consent. Thus, if Joe calls Jane on the telephone, it is legal for Joe to tape the conversation under federal law, and most state law, without first notifying Jane or asking for her permission because one of the parties to the call (*i.e.*, Joe) has consented to the taping. However, some states (*e.g.*, California) require *both* parties to a communication to consent to monitoring.

Telemarketing Sales Rules

The telemarketing sales rules apply to for-profit organizations and charitable solicitations made by for-profit telemarketing vendors. Among other things, the rules require that: (1) calls only be made between 8 a.m. and 9 p.m.; (2) the solicitor display caller ID information; (3) callers identify themselves and what they are selling; and (4) that they honor the wishes of those on the do-not-call registry.

National Do-Not-Call Registry

The do-not-call registry permits citizens who do not want to be contacted by telemarketers to register their residential and wireless phone numbers with the FTC. Telemarketers are required to access the registry before making any phone solicitations and must update their call lists every 31 days to ensure they are up to date.

Customer Proprietary Network Information (CPNI) Rules

In order to provide service, telecommunications providers collect information about their customer such as the numbers they call and when they call them, as well as the particular services they use, such as call forwarding or voice mail. This information is called *Customer Proprietary Network Information* (CPNI) and the *Telecommunications Act of 1996* as well as FCC regulations require telephone companies to protect the confidentiality of this information. Thus, in general, telephone companies may not use, disclose, or permit access to CPNI except: (1) as required by law (*e.g.*, in response to a valid subpoena); (2) with the customer's approval; or (3) in providing the service from which the CPNI is derived (*e.g.*, they can use the information in order to bill the customer for their service).

Fair Credit Reporting Act (FCRA)

The FCRA governs the use of consumer reports. *Consumer reports* include reports containing information that pertains to credit worthiness, credit standing, credit capacity, character, general reputation, personal characteristics, or mode of living that are also used for the purpose of serving as a factor in establishing a consumer's eligibility for credit, insurance, employment, or other business purpose. Among other things, the FCRA requires that consumers receive notice when third-party data is used to make adverse decisions about them, and they must have access to their reports and an opportunity to dispute or correct any errors.

Gramm-Leach-Bliley Act (GLBA)

The GLBA requires financial institutions to protect the personal financial information they hold relating to their provision of financial services to customers and consumers. "Financial institutions" include not only banks, securities firms, and insurance companies, but also companies providing many other types of financial products and services to consumers. The GLBA requires all financial institutions to design, implement, and maintain safeguards to protect customer information. For example, financial institutions must give notice of their policies regarding sharing of personal information and must also give consumers the choice to opt out of some sharing of financial information.

Health Insurance Portability and Accountability Act (HIPAA)

The HIPAA seeks to protect the privacy of electronically transferred health care information. The Department of Health and Human Services has enacted regulations under the HIPAA that contain, among other things, certain requirements for privacy notices, authorizations for use, and disclosure of personal health information, as well as certain security safeguards that covered entities must follow.

Driver's Privacy Protection Act (DPPA)

The DPPA is intended to protect the privacy of personal information gathered by state departments or bureaus of motor vehicles. Accordingly, the DPPA prohibits the release or use of personal information obtained about an individual in connection with a motor vehicle and requires states to get express permission before personal information is given to third-party marketers.

Family Educational Rights and Privacy Act of 1974 (FERPA)

The FERPA puts limits on disclosure of educational records maintained by agencies and institutions that receive federal funding.

Finally, while a discussion of the international law of privacy is beyond the scope of this book, it should be noted that many countries around the globe have enacted their own privacy and data protection laws. For example, in order to prevent the sorts of privacy violations committed in parts of Europe during World War II and the Cold War, the European Union has adopted a series of directives that treat the protection of privacy as a fundamental human right. Accordingly, EU member states must ensure that they pass privacy laws that adhere to these often onerous directives. Importantly, these laws even apply to individuals and entities outside the EU that collect personal data about EU citizens.

Chapter Twenty-Six

Eminent Domain and Zoning

If the government takes someone's property for a governmental purpose, the government must compensate that property owner fairly. The right of the government to take property is the right of *eminent domain*. The government, in fact, does have the right to take property for a public purpose. The mere fact that the government has chosen to take your property does not mean that you as a property owner have to stand by idly. Governmental takings may be challenged.

There has been a fair amount of litigation over the last several years challenging certain governmental takings that were not necessarily motivated by *public need*, but were more motivated by the interest of that governmental authority in acquiring a piece of property and then reselling it for a profit to generate income. That is not an appropriate governmental taking of property.

It's the Law

The government, in fact, does have the right to take property for a public purpose.

The general rule is that there has to be some need for the property. If there is some *bona fide* need for a highway, then obviously the highway has to go somewhere, which means that it may have to go over someone's land. If there happens to be a residential development on that land, then it may be that the government has to take that land, compensate the property owners for the loss of their homes and the expense associated with moving, and then raze those homes to make way for the highway.

The same rationale would apply in regard to acquiring land for parks. Those types of takings are never happy occasions for the government or for the property owners who are affected, but the government has to weigh the general public benefit against the particular detriment to a small number of individuals. If you are one who is subject to a governmental taking, the overall public need or benefit may not seem to be terribly convincing.

Once the government has made a decision to take your property, then under the constitution it is obliged to compensate you fairly for that taking. That compensation is generally based upon a determination of the *fair market value* of your property. When a lawsuit, referred to as an *eminent domain action* or *condemnation action*, is filed by the government agency that condemns or takes your property, the parties are asking the court to determine the fair market value of that property.

The actual taking occurs when the government files a certificate at the courthouse stating it is taking title to the property. Upon the filing of that certificate, the title to that property is transferred to the government. The only issue then to be decided by the court is what the property is worth. That may involve a trial. Different jurisdictions handle these trials in different ways. In some jurisdictions, these types of cases are tried before commissioners.

These commissioners may be local citizens or individuals who have been chosen by the court for having some knowledge or expertise in local property values. The commissioners sit on a jury panel and hear evidence regarding the value of the property and then make a decision as to what the value is. The evidence they hear is testimony from appraisers and perhaps other property owners concerning the piece of property's worth and what economic effect the taking has upon the property owner.

Zoning

Zoning laws are specific to each jurisdiction. Some jurisdictions do not have zoning laws. Typically it is the local government that enacts zoning regulations. The purpose of zoning regulations or laws is to provide some governmental controls over growth and construction within that community. If you are a developer and you happen to buy a five-hundred acre farm wanting to build a housing development on that land, it is obviously going to have a significant impact on the local government in terms of road usage, necessity for schools, requirements for police and fire services, and all sorts of other public services. The local government has a right to have some controls over how many homes are built and how many people will live in that development. The purpose of zoning laws is to provide controls in that regard and many other respects.

Chapter Twenty-Seven

Liens

A *lien* is a security interest that one party has in property that is held by another person. For instance, the mortgage against your family home is a lien. The lien holder is the mortgage company to whom you make your monthly payments. The lien itself is the mortgage or what in some jurisdictions may be referred to as the deed of trust. Both constitute a security interest against your home. The purpose of that lien or security interest is to secure the mortgage company for the payment of the mortgage.

If you fail to make your monthly mortgage payments, then the lien holder—the mortgage company—may foreclose on that lien or mortgage to take the property back and then sell it so that they may recover the money they loaned to you plus their expenses associated with the foreclosure. In the event that you sell the property, your lienholder will be paid in full from the proceeds of the sale, assuming foreclosure brings sufficient funds.

Mechanic's Lien

Liens may also arise in a number of other circumstances. You have probably heard the term *mechanic's lien*. Literally, a mechanic's lien is a type of lien that can be filed by a mechanic, material supplier, or workman who does work on your real estate. For instance, if you hire a contractor to come into your home and add a bedroom and you do not pay that contractor, then that contractor can file a mechanic's lien at the courthouse.

The purpose of that mechanic's lien is to put the rest of the world on notice of the fact that you owe that contractor an amount of money and that the contractor now has a lien or security interest against your property until that debt is paid. If you attempt to sell your property, before any sale could go through you would have to satisfy that mechanic's lien either by paying it off or by placing an amount of money in escrow to cover it in the event the mechanic's lien is found not to be *bona fide*.

Once a mechanic's lien is filed, typically the mechanic (contractor or material supplier) has a designated amount of time within which to file suit against you to enforce the lien. If suit is not filed within the time allowed, then the mechanic's lien is generally considered to be unenforceable although it may not be released of record at the courthouse without further action on your part.

Garagekeeper's Lien

Another type of lien is a *garagekeeper's lien*. If you store your vehicle in a garage for a period of time and then refuse to pay the garagekeeper, then that garagekeeper may have a lien against your vehicle. That lien may entitle the garagekeeper to hold your vehicle until you pay the obligation. Likewise if you take your vehicle to a repair shop for repair and then refuse to pay the bill, the repairperson may have the right to assert a lien against that vehicle. It might entitle the repairperson to hold your vehicle until such time as you pay the repair bill. The mere fact that you paid the repair bill does not mean that you cannot then recoup that amount by suing the repairperson.

Example: If the work is not done properly and the repairman attempts to hold your vehicle hostage pending payment of the bill, then you could go ahead and pay the bill in order to get your vehicle back. You can then sue the repairperson in a civil action in order to recover the money that you had paid for the work that was not properly performed.

Innkeeper's Lien

Another type of lien that may come into existence is an *innkeeper's lien*. If you spend time at a motel and do not pay for the room, then the innkeeper may have a lien against whatever personal property you have on the premises in order to secure the eventual payment of the bill for the room. If you do not pay the bill for the room, then the innkeeper may be entitled to hold that property until the bill is paid.

Domestic Relation's Lien

In domestic relations matters, liens may arise in regard to child support and spousal support. If one spouse does not pay child support or spousal support that is ordered by the court, then by operation of law there may arise a lien against that nonpaying spouse's real estate. That lien will become a matter of public record at the courthouse so that any attempt made by that non-paying spouse to sell his or her real estate would be potentially blocked by the fact that there is a lien against the real estate for the amount of unpaid child support or spousal support.

Attorney's Lien

It's the Law

Attorneys can acquire liens for their services.

Attorneys can likewise acquire liens for their services. If you hire an attorney and refuse to pay for his or her services or dismiss him or her before a settlement or judgement is reached from which he or she could receive payment, the attorney may have an *attorney's lien* against that eventual settlement or judgment amount based upon the reasonable value of his or her services. Although the fee agreement in existence between you and the attorney may have been what is referred to as a *contingent fee agreement*—for one-third or one-fourth of the eventual recovery—if you dismiss the attorney, he or she *may* be entitled to compensation for the reasonable value of the number of hours he or she devoted to the case.

Tax Lien

Another type of lien that may arise is a *tax lien*. If you do not pay your property taxes for your real estate, then the local or state government may record a lien against your property. Likewise, if you do not pay your federal income or estate taxes, the federal government may file an *IRS lien*. Those liens are filed in the same office where the deed to your property is recorded and any attempt by you to sell the property will be impeded unless that lien is satisfied.

Judgment Lien

After a judgment is entered by a court against a defendant, a judgment lien may arise as to property owned by the defendant. While state law and local practice typically differ with respect to the creation of a judgment lien, the mechanics of creating a lien are usually similar. A judgment creditor (*i.e.*, plaintiff) typically first attempts to have the judgment debtor (*i.e.*, defendant) voluntarily satisfy the judgment. If the judgment debtor fails or refuses to voluntarily satisfy the judgment, a judgment lien can be created against the judgment debtor's property.

To create a judgment lien against real property, the judgment creditor typically obtains an Abstract of Judgment from the court that issued the judgment. The Abstract of Judgment lists information about the judgment creditor, the judgment debtor, and the amount of the judgment. The judgment creditor then records the Abstract of Judgment in the land records in the county in which the judgment debtor owns real property. Usually the judgment lien is then satisfied from the sale proceeds when the judgment debtor sells the real property. In the meantime, the judgment creditor has a lien against the property (which in effect secures payment of the judgment) and the outstanding balance of the judgment increases due to the addition of statutory interest on the amount of the judgment which remains unsatisfied.

Secured Transaction

In Chapter 12, reference was made to the Uniform Commercial Code. Part of the Uniform Commercial Code deals with *secured transactions*, which is concerned with the placement and enforcement of liens. The liens governed by this code are security interests. That security interest is obtained by the lender filing a specific document at the courthouse to notify the world that the lender has a security interest in a particular piece of personal property that is at a specific location. The purpose of the filing at the courthouse is to make sure that anybody else who may contemplate buying that piece of property is on notice of the fact that the lender has an interest in it.

Conclusion

As you may have gathered from reading this book, I am *very proud* of being an attorney and *very proud* of how our legal system seeks to protect the rights of all people.

The legal profession is the protector of the unprotected, the advocate for unpopular causes, and the spokesperson for those who cannot speak for themselves. Our Constitution and laws bestow upon each of us certain rights. The legal profession acts as a deterrent to those who might otherwise trample those rights and provides a vehicle for redress for those who have been injured by the unlawful or negligent acts of others. If lawyers did not zealously protect the rights of our citizens, who else would?

One need only look at the serious injuries caused by tobacco, breast implants, or prescription drugs to see that individuals and businesses are in fact accountable to us for injuries they cause by marketing and selling products that are not safe and that cause serious injuries, including death, to members of our society. Without the legal profession there would be no pressure on people and businesses to manufacture and sell safe products, build safe homes and cars, petition for laws to protect us in the workplace, overturn laws that are unfair, and prevent the government from taking our life, liberty, or property without due process of law.

I hope that this book provides you with a better understanding of our system of laws and will become a handy reference for you and your family to consult for many years to come.

Glossary

A

actus reus. A concept in criminal law that involves the criminal act itself.

administrative law. Rules and regulations enacted by local, state, or federal administrative agencies.

Alternative Dispute Resolution. A mechanism by which civil disputes are resolved as an alternative to civil litigation; typically takes the form of arbitration, mediation, or neutral case evaluation.

arbitration. An alternative to a trial before a judge and/or jury. In most arbitrations there is one arbitrator who acts as the judge although in some instances there may be more than one arbitrator who collectively act as the judge or judges to decide the case. Arbitrators act in all instances without a jury.

attractive nuisance. A legal principle that applies in tort law wherein certain objects may be considered to be an attractive nuisance to a child and thereby create liability for the owner or manager of that property.

B

bankruptcy. The filing of a petition in a U.S. Bankruptcy Court claiming that the debtor's liabilities exceed his or her assets.

Bill of Rights.   The first ten Amendments to the U.S. Constitution.

burden of proof. This determines who has the responsibility for proving their case. In a civil action, that burden of proof belongs to the plaintiff who is the party bringing the case. In a criminal case the burden of proof rests with the government to prove guilt beyond a reasonable doubt.

C

case law. Written decisions of trial or appellate courts.

Children's Online Privacy Protection Act. Generally prohibits commercial Web sites and online services from knowingly collecting personal information from children under 13 without parental consent.

civil law. That body of law consisting of statutes, case decisions, and administrative rules and regulations for matters that are noncriminal.

Computer Fraud and Abuse Act. Prohibits unauthorized access to a computer used in interstate or foreign commerce or communication.

consideration. The quid pro quo or tit for tat that constitutes the meat of any agreement or contract.

contract. An agreement to either do or not do something that involves the exchange of some consideration.

contributory negligence. A concept that applies in tort law whereby a plaintiff's claim may be barred if the plaintiff is guilty of any negligence that caused the injury.

Controlling the Assault of Non-Solicited Pornography and Marketing Act. Places certain restrictions on unsolicited email directed to or originating from the U.S. whose primary purpose is advertising or promoting a commercial product or service, including content on a Web site.

criminal law. Statutes enacted by federal, state, or local legislative bodies that impose criminal penalties for certain actions. The criminal penalty may consist of being imprisoned or being fined.

cross-examination. The questioning of a witness by the opposing attorney.

customer proprietary network information. Data collected by telecommunications providers about a consumer's telephone calls, such as the numbers they call and when they call them, as well as the particular services they use. Telephone companies may not use, disclose, or permit access to this data except under certain circumstances.

D

defamation. A false statement made about someone or some organization that is damaging to their reputation.

discovery. The process by which each party involved in litigation may discover the facts and circumstances surrounding the other party's case.

direct examination. The questioning of a witness by the attorney who calls that witness as part of his case.

diversity jurisdiction. An element of subject matter jurisdiction in federal court that requires that there must be a diversity of citizenship between opposite parties in the case.

double jeopardy. A constitutional principle that prohibits a person from being tried twice for the same crime.

Driver's Privacy Protection Act. Protects the privacy of personal information gathered by state departments or bureaus of motor vehicles.

E

Electronic Fund Transfer Act. Provides consumer protection for all transactions using a debit card or electronic means to debit or credit an account and also limits a consumer's liability for unauthorized electronic fund transfers.

equitable distribution. The distribution of marital assets as part of a divorce proceeding.

equitable relief. One party asking the court to prohibit the other party from doing something or mandating that the other party do something.

evidence. Evidence can come in many different forms but typically it comes in the form of testimony, documents, and other physical exhibits.

exclusionary rule. A rule of evidence that applies in criminal cases whereby evidence may be excluded if it was improperly obtained by the law enforcement authorities.

F

Fair Credit Billing Act. Establishes procedures for resolving billing errors on your credit card accounts and also limits a consumer's liability for fraudulent credit card charges.

Fair Credit Reporting Act. Establishes procedures for correcting mistakes on your credit record and requires that your record only be provided for legitimate business needs.

Fair Debt Collection Practices Act. Prohibits debt collectors from using unfair or deceptive practices to collect overdue bills that your creditor has forwarded for collection.

Family Educational Rights and Privacy Act. Places limits on disclosure of educational records maintained by agencies and institutions that receive federal funding.

felony. A crime for which a person may be imprisoned for more than a year.

G

Gramm-Leach-Bliley Act. Requires financial institutions to protect the personal financial information they hold relating to their provision of financial services to customers and consumers.

H

Health Insurance Portability and Accountability Act. Protects the privacy of electronically transferred health care information by mandating certain requirements for privacy notices, authorizations for use and disclosure of personal health information, as well as certain security safeguards.

hearsay. An out of court statement that is offered for its truth value.

I

Identity Theft and Assumption Deterrence Act. Makes identity theft a federal crime.

J

judgment lien. A lien on the property of a debtor resulting from a court's judgment.

L

Lanham Trademark Act. Contains the federal statutes of trademark law in the United States and generally prohibits trademark infringement, trademark dilution, and false advertising.

legal relief. Legal relief typically involves the award of some money damages in the form of a money judgment against the defendant.

lien. A security interest one person has in the property of another. The most common security interest is a mortgage or deed of trust for a piece of real estate.

M

mediation. An informal, and usually voluntary, form of Alternative Dispute Resolution presided over by a neutral party whose sole objective is to help the parties reach a settlement.

mens rea. A concept in criminal law that involves criminal intent on the part of the defendant.

Miranda **rights.** Rights that apply in a criminal investigation to a potential suspect to be advised of his or her right to remain silent and right to counsel.

misdemeanor. A crime for which a person may be imprisoned for up to a year.

N

National Do-Not-Call Registry. Permits citizens who do not want to be contacted by telemarketers to register their residential and wireless phone numbers with the FTC.

negligence. The failure to exercise ordinary care in a particular circumstance.

neutral case evaluation. A form of Alternative Dispute Resolution designed to provide some guidance to the parties as to how their dispute may be resolved. The evaluation reached by the neutral case evaluator is purely a recommendation intended to serve as a guide to the parties in evaluating the case.

P

parol evidence. A rule of evidence that applies in regard to contract litigation that may exclude the admission of certain evidence unless it is part of the written contract.

personal jurisdiction. This applies to whether the court has jurisdiction over the defendants in a civil case.

premises liability. A theory of liability in tort law by which a property owner or manager may be liable to persons who are on the premises.

privilege. Legal protection that may apply to certain relationships, for instance the attorney/client relationship or the doctor/patient relationship.

probable cause. A legal principle that governs justification for making an arrest or issuing an arrest or search warrant. Probable cause means that it is reasonably probable that the person has committed a crime or that evidence of the crime may be on the premises.

product liability. A theory of tort law by which a manufacturer or seller of a product may be liable for injuries resulting from the product.

professional liability. Liability of a professional person to a client or patient.

proof. Proof comes in the form of evidence. Evidence comes in the form of testimony, documents, and physical things that are likely to prove the truth or falsity of an issue in the case.

property settlement agreement. A contract or agreement entered into between husband and wife resolving all disputes relating to the marriage.

proximate cause. A concept in tort law by which a negligent or intentional act is deemed to be the near cause of damages as opposed to the remote cause.

R

relevance. Something is relevant if it tends to prove or disprove an issue in the case.

res ipsa loquitur. A principle that applies in tort law wherein the jury may infer that the defendant is negligent if an event occurs involving an item that is within the defendant's exclusive control and it typically would not have caused injury to the plaintiff but for some negligence on the part of the defendant.

S

single act jurisdiction. A principle of jurisdiction whereby a single act directed at a company or resident in a particular state *may* subject a person outside the state to being sued in that state's courts.

spam. Unsolicited electronic mail, usually sent in bulk for commercial or marketing purposes.

standard of care. A legal principle that applies in negligence cases and governs whether conduct of the defendant is up to the standard that applies to the reasonably prudent practitioner in that profession.

standard of proof. The level of proof that is required in a criminal or civil case. In a civil case the standard of proof is typically what is called the preponderance of the evidence. In a criminal case the standard of proof is typically proof beyond a reasonable doubt.

statute of frauds. A defense that may apply in regard to contract litigation whereby certain contracts are considered not to be enforceable unless they are in writing.

statutory law. Laws created by state, federal, or local legislative bodies.

strict liability. A principle in tort law wherein a defendant may be held liable even though there is no evidence of negligence. Such an activity may include a blasting case wherein blasting activities cause damage to an adjoining property owner.

subject matter jurisdiction. This governs the authority of a court to hear particular types of cases.

V
voir dire. The questioning of potential jurors before a trial to determine if they have any biases.

W
will. A legal document signed by a living human being directing the disposition of his or her assets upon his or her death.

Wiretap Act. Prohibits the government and individuals from intentionally intercepting, using, or disclosing wire, oral, or electronic communications, except under certain circumstances.

workers' compensation. A legal system created either by state or federal law providing for the award of lost income, medical expenses, and other benefits to persons who are injured on the job.

wrongful death action. A type of tort action that is brought wherein the injured party has died as a result of the fault of the defendant.

Index

S

W

Y

Z

About the Authors

Brien A. Roche is a practicing attorney in Virginia, Maryland, and Washington, D.C. He has been practicing law since 1976. He is a graduate of Georgetown University and a graduate of the George Washington University Law School. After college, he served in the United States Marine Corps, and thereafter served as a patrol officer with the Washington, D.C., police department (known as the Metropolitan Police Department of Washington, D.C.).

Since 1976, Mr. Roche has been engaged in the general practice of law in the tri-state area surrounding Washington, D.C. Licensed in Virginia, Maryland, and the District of Columbia, his litigation practice incorporates all facets of the law.

He is the author of two professional legal texts that are published by Lexis Publishing Company. *The Virginia Tort Case Finder* is a title well-recognized by Virginia lawyers and judges. The second book, *The Virginia Domestic Relations Case Finder*, is a must-have reference for all family law practicioners in the state of Virginia. He has also coauthored a book entitled *Objections: Interrogatories, Depositions, and Trial*, which is published by the Virginia Law Foundation.

In addition, Mr. Roche has also authored several articles in legal publications and has lectured at numerous continuing legal education seminars around the state of Virginia.

He is the proud father of the two coauthors and their five siblings.

John K. Roche is a practicing attorney in Virginia and Washington, D.C. He has been practicing law since 2004 with the firm of Perkins Coie LLP. He is a graduate of Georgetown University and a graduate of the College of William & Mary Law School. Mr. Roche is a member of Perkins Coie's Commercial Litigation group and the firm's Privacy & Security Law group. He focuses his practice on commercial litigation and counseling, particularly in the areas of intellectual property, privacy, security, Internet, communications, and employment law. He lives in Fairfax County with his wife, Kyle, and their two daughters.

Sean P. Roche is a practicing attorney in Virginia and Washington, D.C. He has been practicing law since 2005 with the firm of Odin, Feldman & Pittleman, P.C. He is a graduate of Georgetown University and the University of Richmond School of Law. At the University of Richmond, Mr. Roche was a member of the *University of Richmond Law Review*. Mr. Roche is a member of Odin Feldman's Civil/Commercial Litigation group. He lives in Arlington, Virginia, with his wife, Rebecca, and their very large yellow lab, Charlie.